# ACKNOWLEDGEMENTS

I would like to thank:

Mychelle Blake for being my e-mail tech help, grammatical support line and sanity-preserver. You really do have a twisted sense of humor.

Laura Bourhenne for manuscript review with your usual sharp eye, and for being such a fun radio show co-host. And yes, you are *exactly right!*

Paul Owens for manuscript review and insightful comments, not to mention all those stress-relieving, sugar-laden-dessert lunches.

Daniel Terry, my father, for proofreading and suggestions. And thanks, Mom, for keeping a leash on him when he goes overboard. Now I know where the good training genes come from.

C.C., my best friend and the light of my life, for your love and support. The printed word could never convey what you mean to me.

Mojo (my beautiful cover boy) and Soko, my fur-kids, for making Mommy happy and keeping me sane when I most need it. There's no better stress-reliever than tummy-rubs!

# Table of Contents

# Part III: Opportunity Knocks, but Business Calls!

# Part IV: Solving the Mystery: Taking a History

## Chapter Thirteen

## Chapter Fourteen

## Chapter Fifteen

# Part V: The Session

## Chapter Sixteen

**Chapter Seventeen**

**Obedience Lesson Guidelines**................................................145

**Chapter Eighteen**

**Protocols and Suggestions**................................................151

# Part VI: Questions, Answers and Other Helpful Stuff

**Chapter Nineteen**

**Commonly Asked Questions**................................................159

**Chapter Twenty**

**Endnote**................................................173

A few notes about terms used in this book:

Canines are referred to as "he" rather than "it." Although not technically correct, dogs are not objects and I refuse to refer to them as such. Grammar Police, take me away!

Owners are referred to as "she." This implies no gender bias, and is simply an alternative to the traditional use of "he" where a pronoun of this type is required.

The word "cue" is used in place of the traditional "command" (a word used when one wishes a dog to perform a specific behavior). "Cue" implies a request rather than a demand, and is more in line with positive, modern training philosophy.

"Lesson," "session" and "appointment" are used interchangeably.

# *Introduction*

If you delight in creative puzzle-solving, enjoy training, and like spending time with people and dogs, private training might be right for you. There are so many aspects to enjoy: discovering what lies at the root of a dog's behavior problem; working closely with a client/dog team to design a protocol; teaching new skills; and best of all, achieving success! Private training is the main focus of my business—and I love it.

Given all of the above, you might think I would be delighted to write about the daily ins and outs of private training. I have to confess, I almost didn't write this book. In 2001 I wrote *So You Want to be a Dog Trainer*, a guide to starting a dog training business. In 2003 came *It's Not the Dogs, It's the People*, a trainer's guide to dealing with the human half of the equation. A lot of information contained in those books is applicable to in-home, one-on-one training. I saw no need for a separate manual on teaching private lessons.

Then I started hearing things; or I should say, seeing things. Online training discussions contained posts about topics such as what to ask when taking a history, or how to handle specific issues like working with two dogs at once. In e-mails, trainers asked advice on everything from how to structure an in-home session, to how to work effectively with elderly clients. Some requests came from new trainers; others, from those who had been teaching group classes for years and now wanted to begin private training. All things considered, it seemed that a manual specifically geared toward in-home trainers was in order.

In this book you will find some topics that have been covered more extensively in my previous books. In those cases, I have referenced the particular book so those who are interested can pursue the topic in greater detail. But even where topics overlap, they are covered differently here. For example, the section on Phone Skills includes a brief description of the Comparison Shopper, as did *So You Want to be a Dog Trainer*. But here you will find sample phone scripts that illustrate exactly *how* to handle problem callers. And although gauging whether you are ready to train professionally has been touched on previously, here you will find specific exercises to help in the self-assessment process.

There is also a lot of fresh, new material in this book. You will find an extensive section on specific questions to ask when taking a history, a point-by-point explanation of how to interpret the answers you receive, and how that information might ultimately help to solve a dog's behavior problems. There are step-by-step instructions on how to structure a private lesson, a section of commonly asked questions (many of which have never been addressed before in print) and much more. As usual, I have included tips and suggestions throughout that you can apply immediately.

Whether you are just starting out as a trainer or adding private lessons to your roster of services, I wish you the very best of luck. I hope you will enjoy private training as much as I do.

*Nicole Wilde*

Part One

# Getting Started

# *Are You Ready?*

If you are just embarking on your career as a professional trainer, or specifically as a private trainer, you may be wondering: *Am I qualified to do this type of work? Is it ethical for me to charge fees when I have limited experience? What if I can't solve a dog's problem? What if someone asks a question I can't answer?* Relax. You're not alone. Every trainer feels some insecurity at first; your confidence will increase with experience. For now, put your worries aside. The exercises in this chapter are designed to help you determine objectively whether you are ready to begin private training.

*What is your Education?*

There is no degree or license required to call oneself a professional dog trainer. As a result, levels of education and experience vary widely in the industry. Some trainers have more "book knowledge," while others have many years of hands-on experience. Many of the best trainers have both. Although familiarity with the psychology behind how dogs learn is not a prerequisite to training a dog, understanding and applying it will make you a better trainer. Knowing the lingo is also helpful in discussions with other trainers.

The following exercise is designed to gauge your knowledge of theory and its application to training, and basic training techniques.

## Exercise One: Theory and Technique

*Write out (or type) your answers to the questions that follow. The answers can be found at the end of the exercise—but don't peek until you have finished!*

1. Briefly explain the difference between classical and operant conditioning.

2. What are the four quadrants of operant conditioning?

3. Define each quadrant and give an example of how it could be applied to training. (Even if you choose not to use all four quadrants in training, you should still understand the principles and applications of each.)

4. In what type of circumstance might you apply classical conditioning, and how?

5. Name two types of schedules of reinforcement and briefly explain each.

6. What is a conditioned reinforcer and how is it used?

7. Define "luring" and give an example of how it could be used to train a behavior.

8. Define "shaping" and give an example of how it could be used to train a behavior.

**Answers:**

1. *Classical conditioning* involves creating associations. The classic example is Pavlov's experiment, where the ringing of a bell was immediately followed by the presentation of food; the dog eventually came to associate the sound of the bell with food, and would salivate at the sound of the bell.

   *Operant conditioning* is about consequences. The dog is rewarded or punished for a behavior, thereby increasing or decreasing the future incidence of that behavior.

2. The four quadrants of operant conditioning are: positive reinforcement (+R), negative reinforcement (-R), positive punishment (+P) and negative punishment (-P).

3. *Positive reinforcement* is the presentation of something the dog perceives as rewarding. Example: dog is asked to sit, dog sits, dog receives treat.

   *Negative reinforcement* is the removal of something the dog perceives as unpleasant. Example: the stimulation of an electronic collar (which I do not use nor recommend, with the possible exception of extreme cases such as rattlesnake avoidance training) is turned off when the dog complies with a request.

   *Positive punishment* is the presentation of something the dog perceives as unpleasant. Example: dog pulls on leash, choke chain correction is administered. (I do not use nor recommend choke chains.)
   *Note*: Positive punishment ranges from mild to harsh. Even a verbal correction could technically be termed "positive punishment."

   *Negative punishment* is the removal of something the dog perceives as rewarding. Example: dog nips, human leaves the room. This is a "time out," which punishes the dog by removing valued social contact.

4. Classical conditioning is most often employed to change a dog's associations with—and therefore underlying emotional reaction toward—something or someone. For example, a dog is fearful of unfamiliar dogs. Each time the dog sees another dog, he is presented with a handful of hot dogs (assuming this particular dog loves hot dogs). Eventually, the dog learns that the presence of unfamiliar dogs predicts the appearance of hot dogs. The dog's attitude toward new dogs eventually changes from fear to happy anticipation.

5. *Continuous reinforcement* means a dog gets rewarded *each time* he performs a behavior correctly. This type of schedule is almost always used while a dog is learning a new behavior (some trainers prefer to continue this schedule indefinitely). *Variable reinforcement* means the dog gets rewarded *some* of the time he performs a behavior correctly. Think "Las Vegas slot machine" and you'll see why the dog keeps playing the game on a variable reinforcement schedule.

Other types of reinforcement schedules also exist, including *differential* and *intermittent*. (For more information, see *Appendix C*, Theories & Principles of Behavior.)

6.  A *conditioned reinforcer*, also known as a "bridging stimulus" or "marker," is a signal that is given at the exact moment a dog performs a desired behavior. This marker is immediately followed by a reward, which is how the marker becomes "conditioned" as a "reinforcer" in and of itself. The clicker is a commonly used conditioned reinforcer in dog training, as well as in training exotic animals. (For more information on clicker training, see *Appendix C*, Clicker Training.)

7.  *Luring* means coaxing a dog into position by having him follow a *lure*, usually a food treat. To lure a dog from a sit into a down, you would hold the treat to the dog's nose like a magnet, move it in a straight line down to the ground, then if necessary, pull the treat along the ground slightly toward you. (The full motion would look like tracing a capital letter "L.") A successful lure is followed by a reward; in this case, the treat.

8.  *Shaping* means breaking a behavior down and rewarding small progressive bits, or *successive approximations*, to achieve a goal. To shape a down from a sit, for example, you would first reward the dog for any lowering of the head. You would then hold out for a lower head dip, then lower, until the dog's head was at ground level, rewarding each bit of progress along the way. You might then reward one paw moving forward, then two, and so on until the dog is lying flat. Using a marker such as a clicker is helpful when shaping behaviors, since it precisely marks the instant the desired piece of behavior takes place.

If you were already familiar with these theories and techniques, great! If, on the other hand, you glanced at the questions and thought, *What* is *that mumbo-jumbo?*, don't worry. There is plenty of information available. Two good books to start with are *Don't Shoot the Dog* by Karen Pryor and *Excel-erated Learning* by Pamela Reid. (See *Appendix C*, Theories and Principles of Behavior for further suggestions.)

*What is Your Hands-on Experience?*

How many dogs have you actually worked with? If your answer is, "I trained my own dog," that's a good start—but it is not sufficient experience with which to begin training clients' dogs. On the other hand, if you have volunteered at a shelter or rescue organization for some time and have worked hands-on with various breeds and temperaments, you already have some solid experience.

Perhaps you have apprenticed under another trainer who teaches private lessons. If so, you probably have an idea of how to structure sessions, what questions to ask, and how to handle problems that arise during a session. If you have assisted in or taught group classes, you already know how to train obedience exercises and have probably gained skills in dealing with people as well. (For in-depth information on dealing with people in both group classes and private lessons, see *It's Not the Dogs, It's the People!* in *Appendix C,* Dealing with Clients.) If you feel you need further hands-on experience, the good news is that regardless of where you live or your level of income, there are opportunities to explore. The end of this chapter explores some of those options, with specific contact information listed in *Appendix C.*

*Training Basic Behaviors*

If you are experienced in teaching basic obedience, you already have an advantage as far as teaching private lessons. There are plenty of owners who just want their dogs to stop pulling on leash or to come when called. Basic obedience skills can also be used to solve behavior issues. For example, a dog who jumps on visitors could be taught to go to bed and lie down whenever the doorbell rings. If you already know how to teach "go to bed" and down-stay, you would simply add the doorbell as a cue.

Since not all dogs learn and respond to training in the same way, the more techniques (and modifications to those techniques) you know, the better. For example, when being taught to lie down from a sitting position, Muffin the Maltese does not respond to attempts to lure the down in one smooth motion. You have tried it three times and still Muffin just sits there staring at you as though you've sprouted antlers. What now? Will you tell her owner that Muffin is obviously half-baked and move on? Hopefully not.

If you are familiar with shaping (see Answer 8, Exercise One), you could shape the down. Alternately, you could sit on the floor with one knee slightly raised and lure Muffin under that knee by placing a treat on the side opposite her, thereby forcing her to lie down in order to reach the treat. Or, you could *capture* the desired behavior by waiting for Muffin to lie down on her own, then rewarding her. You could even position Muffin so she is sitting on a stair or table, then move the treat below that level so that in order to get it, she *has* to lie down.

Five different methods to teach a dog to lie down have been mentioned: luring from a sit, shaping, capturing, luring under the knee, and the stair/table lure. You do not need to know five ways to teach every obedience behavior, but you should be familiar with at least one or two alternatives.

**Exercise Two: Basic Behaviors—What's in Your Bag of Tricks?**

*Following is a list of common basic obedience behaviors, along with a few other skills you should know how to teach dogs. Write or type as many ways as you know to train each one.*

---

### Group A: Basic Behaviors

Watch (a.k.a. Attention, Name Recognition)
Sit
Down
Stay (Sit-Stay, Down-Stay)
Come
Walk Nicely on Leash (a.k.a. "Loose Leash Walking," as opposed to a strict obedience competition-style "Heel")

---

---

**Group B:  H.I.R.E.**
**(Helpful In Real-Life Environments) Skills**

Leave It (Back off)
Drop It  ("Kindly spit out that thing in your mouth!")
Go to Bed (or place)
Off (furniture)
Wait (This can range from "wait until released to eat a
meal" to an emergency "WAIT!" as the dog is bolting
down the street. It means "be motionless" but is of
shorter duration than a Stay.)

---

Unfortunately, it is not possible to list answers to this exercise, as
instructions for teaching these exercises would merit a book in itself—
and there are many good ones on the market. (See *Appendix C,* Training
Basic Obedience.)

How did you do on the exercise? If you knew at least one and perhaps
two ways to teach each skill, you're doing great! You will pick up
additional techniques as you read, attend seminars, network with other
trainers, and experiment on your own. If you were unsure as to how to
train any particular behavior, especially those in Group A, you will need
to improve your training skills before instructing others in private lessons.

*Behavior Issues*

Private lessons often involve solving behavior issues. Based on your
knowledge and hands-on experience, will you feel comfortable addressing
all issues, or will you set limits? Behavior issues range from mild (stealing
food from countertops, jumping on people) to severe (intense aggression,
clinical separation anxiety). The latter two can be challenging to work
with, not only intellectually, but emotionally. The success of a behavior
modification program can literally mean life or death for a dog.
Completing the self-assessment exercises in this chapter will help you to
determine which issues you feel ready and/or willing to tackle.

You do not have to accept every behavior case that comes your way. In fact, it would be a huge mistake to take on complex issues until you have the expertise and confidence to do so. There is nothing wrong with referring a case to another trainer or behavior specialist. It is the mark of a good trainer to know what she can and can not realistically handle. Attempting to handle an issue for which you are not qualified can have devastating consequences for both dog and owner, not to mention your own safety and reputation. You can always take on serious behavior issues once you have a few years of experience under your belt; and should you decide you never want to deal with them, that is also perfectly acceptable. I know many trainers who have built thriving businesses without ever handling severe behavior issues. Never let anyone pressure you into taking a case for which you are not prepared.

Now that you have been duly whacked over the head with the gravity of taking on serious behavior issues before you are ready, let's lighten things up. The following exercise begins with milder behavior issues. Since some (e.g., jumping on visitors and housebreaking) are extremely common, knowing how to address them is a must.

### Exercise Three: Behavior Issues

This exercise will help to assess which issues you are knowledgeable and experienced with, and feel confident to address. Take your time and consider your answers carefully. The exercise might even take a few days to complete, but it will be well worth the effort. In addition to the results offering a valuable assessment of your knowledge and experience, taking the exercise will help to clarify your approach and techniques. And if you save your answers on a computer, you will have files to refer to any time these issues arise. As with the previous exercise, space does not allow for the inclusion of answers; but behavior issues are covered extensively in books listed throughout *Appendix C*.

*Explain how you would address each of the issues listed on the following page, using both management and training. Include topics to be covered and information to impart to the owner.*

Jumping on family members      Housebreaking/crate training
Jumping on visitors            Yard escaping
Jumping on furniture           Door-darting (bolting out doors)
Chewing/destruction            Digging
Stealing items/"keep-away"     Barking
Nipping
Attention-seeking (e.g., pawing, whining)
Counter-surfing (stealing from countertops)

*Although the following are broad issues and solutions will vary depending on the specific situation, there are some basic principles and methods that can generally be applied. If you do not plan to handle aggression or other complex behavior issues, skip this section:*

Separation anxiety
Fears and phobias
Obsessive-compulsive disorders

Aggression toward strangers (in home/on walks)
Aggression toward family member(s)
Aggression toward unfamiliar dogs (on-leash/off-leash)
Dog-dog aggression within household
Predatory aggression (e.g., toward family cat)
Resource guarding (e.g., food, valued items, locations)

If you felt confident addressing the majority of these issues, great! If not, this is the perfect opportunity to research areas in which you feel uncertain.

*Furthering Your Education*

Reading books, watching videos and attending seminars all provide opportunities to learn about theory, training techniques and behavior modification. Apprenticing with another trainer is even better. This relationship allows you to observe the trainer's approach and techniques, and ask questions along the way. If there is a trainer whose skills and methods you admire, ask whether she might consider taking on an apprentice.

You could attend a school or workshop, such as the San Francisco SPCA's Academy for Dog Trainers. While some schools or courses last only a week or two, others are more in-depth and take months to complete. If being away from home for long periods presents a problem, there are alternatives. Many expert instructors conduct workshops around the country to train trainers. If your area does not get many workshops, you could ask whether a speaker would be willing to travel to your area if you host one yourself—you provide the venue and guarantee a fee and/or specified number of attendees. (See *Appendix C,* Schools, Train-the-Trainer Seminars and Internship Opportunities.)

An excellent way to assess and improve your existing skills is to view videotape of yourself teaching. Yes, I know, most of us hate to watch ourselves—but it can be an immensely helpful tool. Ask one friend to handle the video camera (or set it on a tripod), and another to play the owner. Act as naturally as possible when instructing dog and owner. Explain the exercise and demonstrate with the dog, then give feedback as the owner practices. Don't be too hard on yourself when watching the playback, but do try to pinpoint areas that need improvement. Your interaction with the dog might point to a need for improved technique, better timing, or clearer body language. Your communication with the "owner" might highlight a lack of clarity, patience, or positive reinforcement. Use the tape as a learning tool. But just as we do with dogs, be sure to notice all the things you did right!

One of the best things you can do to expand your education is to join the Association of Pet Dog Trainers (APDT). Membership in this worldwide organization entitles you to receive the newsletter *The APDT Chronicle of the Dog* (a bimonthly publication filled with educational articles, book reviews and all manner of helpful information), discounts on books and other products, and a member directory. Membership also entitles you to join the APDT e-mail discussion list, which affords access to experienced, professional trainers who share information, answer questions, and learn from and support each other. (The list, along with the APDT's website—see *Resources*—is also a good source of information on schools, apprenticeships and employment opportunities.) The APDT annual conference is the place to hear some of the world's top trainers and behavior specialists present lectures and workshops. The conference is also a great place to network with other trainers and learn about the latest training products—all in an exciting, whirlwind five days.

As previously stated, no license is required for dog trainers. There is, however, a national certification test offered by the Certification Council for Pet Dog Trainers. (For contact information, see *Resources*.) Upon passing, one earns the title "Certified Pet Dog Trainer" and the right to use the initials CPDT after one's name. I know a few trainers who, once they passed the CPDT exam, felt more at ease presenting themselves as professional trainers. Trainers must earn continuing education credits in order to keep the designation.

Whichever path to knowledge you choose, education should be a life-long pursuit. The very best trainers never feel they "know it all."

Next, we'll ease your transition into the world of professional in-home training.

*2*

# Easing the Transition

*Cheat Sheets*

Early in my career, I developed a useful technique: during my conversation with a caller, I would take notes and create a list of the dog's specific issues. I would then peruse my books and files for pertinent information on each issue. That information would be consolidated into "cheat sheets" that would be carried along to the session.

Each cheat sheet contained questions to ask and important points to cover on a specific topic. These sheets proved invaluable, as it is easy to forget details when you are nervous or caught up in conversation. I had one sheet on topics to cover at a puppy training session; another on exercises to include in a temperament test; and individual sheets for specific behavior problems.

Here is an example of a cheat sheet:

Housebreaking: Questions

How long has the house-soiling been going on?
Is the dog crate trained?
Was any previous housebreaking done and if so, what was
done specifically, by who, and how long ago?
Where does the dog sleep?
Does the dog have accidents overnight?
At what times is the dog fed, and how long is the food left down?
Is water always available?
Where is the dog kept when no one is home?
How many hours on average is the dog left alone?
If the dog is indoors when someone is home, is he restricted to a
certain area?
Where is the preferred spot for the dog to eliminate?

What is the substrate on which the dog eliminates (e.g., grass, concrete, dirt)?
If the dog eliminates in the yard, does someone go out with him?
If so, is the dog on-leash or off-leash?
(If the dog lives in a townhome/apartment) How often is he walked?
Does the walk end directly after the dog eliminates?
When the dog has accidents, where do they happen (what location and on what surface)?
Do these accidents involve urination, defecation or both?
Who is present when the accidents occur?
What is your reaction when catching the dog in the act?
What is your reaction when finding an accident after the fact?
What is being used to clean carpeting/other surfaces?

## Housebreaking: Points to Cover

- Daily schedule of humans (as applicable to management)
- Providing periodic elimination opportunities
- Establishing a verbal cue (e.g., "Go potty!")
- Keeping a log of times at which the dog has defecated
- Praising the dog immediately after elimination, rewarding (if using treats) immediately rather than upon returning indoors
- Management: Crate training, tethering, baby gates, puppy pen (instructions for use when away and when home)
- Proper reaction when catching an accident in progress (and why not to use physical punishment), how to follow up
- Not correcting the dog when finding an "accident" that has already happened
- Cleaning solutions
- Times dogs normally need to urinate (upon waking, after naps, after play, after eating/drinking)
- What is normal to expect time-wise/setbacks

## Exercise: Cheat Sheets

Turn to the previous chapter and choose a behavior topic from Exercise Three. Create a cheat sheet of questions to ask and points to cover.

Begin a file for cheat sheets. Bring those that are applicable to training sessions. At each session, once you have consulted with the client and designed a protocol, review your cheat sheets. It is perfectly fine to say to a client, "I'm just going over my checklist to be sure we covered everything." Clients will appreciate your attention to detail, and you will feel confident that you have addressed the subject comprehensively. If you realize after the fact that a significant point was omitted, call the client. There is no need to feel badly; you do not have to say, "Darn, I forgot to tell you something." Just say there was something else you thought of that would be helpful. Most people will be grateful that you took the time to call. As you gain experience your dependence on cheat sheets will lessen, and eventually, you will not need them at all.

*Butterflies are Just Bugs*

Perhaps after assessing your level of skill and knowledge, you feel you are ready to start your in-home training career. Yet somehow, those butterflies in your stomach disagree. What specifically is making you hesitate? Are you afraid someone will ask a question you cannot answer? There is nothing wrong with telling clients you don't know an answer, but will do some research and get back to them. Most people will appreciate your honesty, as opposed to someone who pretends to know it all. If you network with other trainers, you already have a good source of fact-checking and brainstorming. Even if you do not know other trainers personally, help is available via the internet; the APDT e-mail list is a particularly good resource in this regard. Conferring with other trainers as questions arise will help to increase your knowledge base and confidence.

Is it possible that you have "all the right stuff" including information sources in place but are simply nervous about taking the first step? That feeling is completely normal. Don't let it stop you! One way to build your confidence and ease the transition to paid training is to offer free or discounted sessions to those who adopt from local rescue groups or shelters. That way you are helping adopted dogs while gaining experience, without the pressure of wondering whether you are ready to charge full price for your services. Personally, I did so much free in-home training for a local rescue group before starting to charge for my services, that it became apparent after a while even to me that I ought to start charging a fee. You will know when you are ready. (Note: Many experienced trainers continue to offer discounted services to those who adopt from rescue groups or shelters. I encourage you to do the same.)

It is important that you exude an air of confidence. No one wants to follow a leader who appears hesitant or unsure. Have you ever heard the phrase, "Act *as if*"? Applied to training clients and their dogs, that means *acting* confident even if you do not *feel* confident. Speak with authority and move in an assured manner. Acting *as if* you are confident eventually leads to *being* confident. If you know of a trainer who acts in a self-assured, authoritative manner, pretend you *are* that trainer as you work with clients. That confident manner will eventually become a real part of your persona.

Not only is it absolutely normal to feel hesitant at first, it is also quite common to second-guess yourself frequently early in your career. The sequence usually goes like this: you feel unsure, maybe even fraudulent, presenting yourself as a professional trainer when you do not know as much or have as much experience as other trainers. But you take a deep breath and take the plunge. Soon you have gained a bit of confidence. Things go smoothly for days and even weeks at a time. You are becoming a confident trainer! It's smooth sailing from here on in! …That's usually right about the time you get the case that makes you throw up your hands and think, *Aargh, I don't know anything after all!* That's okay. It's actually good when those things happen—they'll keep you humble. As you continue, setbacks will become fewer and the times between them longer. You will eventually, without even realizing it, have developed into a confident, accomplished trainer.

# Part II

# Da
# Bizness

| Setting Fees |
| Singles vs. Packages |
| The Foundation |

# 3

# The Business of Training

After careful evaluation, you have determined that you are ready to begin your career as a private trainer. But before you take on your first client, take a moment to check that these crucial business components are in place:

1. *Business License* Depending on where you live, you might be required to obtain a business license. Check local statutes through your city or county Business Affairs office.

2. *DBA (Doing Business As)* Regardless of whether you are required to obtain a license, you must run a DBA ad in a local newspaper to announce your business as a formal entity. Call the Classifieds department of your local newspaper for more information.

3. *Incorporation* Whether you run your business as a sole proprietorship or hire employees will determine in part what form your organization should take. If you are a one-person company, you may list your business as a sole proprietorship or a limited liability corporation (LLC). One advantage to the LLC is that should you be sued, only company assets would be a viable target—your personal assets would be protected. There are advantages and disadvantages to incorporation, depending on the size of your company, fees and other factors. State laws vary. Consult with an attorney to choose the most advantageous structure for your company.

4. *Liability Insurance* When I started my business, purchasing insurance never crossed my mind. I thought, *I'm just an in-home trainer, it's not as though I run a large facility or have employees. Who needs the expense!* Then a few years later, I read about a well-known canine behaviorist who was working with a dog in public. The dog bit a

passerby and the behaviorist was sued. He lost—to the tune of one million dollars! Good thing he was insured. Hopefully you will never find it necessary to make an insurance claim, but you will rest easier knowing that should an accident occur, your financial and personal assets are protected. (See *Resources* for insurance companies that write policies specifically for dog trainers.)

5. *Liability Contract*  Although a liability contract might not actually hold up in court, it is crucial to have clients sign one. If nothing else, the simple act of having signed a contract might dissuade a client from filing a lawsuit. *Appendix A* includes sample contracts that include liability clauses. You may use them in their entirety or alter them to fit your needs; either way, be sure to have all contracts reviewed by an attorney, since liability laws vary from state to state.

6. *Resale License*  A resale license is required if you intend to sell products to your clients. Along with a resale license comes the responsibility of annual reporting of sales tax. Contact your state's Board of Equalization for further information.

7. *Bank Account*  Be sure to open a savings/checking account specifically for your training business, no matter how small your initial income. It is much easier to track finances and calculate taxes if you keep your training income and expenses separate from your personal funds.

8. *Accounting Software*  Unless you are married to the custom of doing your accounting by hand, purchase a quality accounting software program such as *Quickbooks*™. It will help you to track income and expenses, generate invoices, and even assist in figuring your taxes. Be sure to back up data regularly!

| | |
|---|---|
| Business License | ____ |
| DBA | ____ |
| Incorporation | ____ |
| Liability Insurance | ____ |
| Liability Contract | ____ |
| Resale License | ____ |
| Bank Account | ____ |
| Accounting Software | ____ |

*4*

# Setting Fees

When you are just starting out, setting fees can seem a daunting task. Although you have gotten over the hump of feeling justified in charging for your services, you may still feel uneasy charging rates comparable to those of more experienced trainers. Then again, if you charge too little, people might not take you seriously; and you might not make enough money to stay in business. What's a trainer to do?

*What the Market will Bear*

Your first order of business is to find out what other trainers in your area charge. There is no such thing as a "standard rate" for dog training; you can only charge what the market will bear in your own service area. Whereas owners living in an upscale urban neighborhood might not think twice about paying $90 per hour, residents of a tiny, rural town might only be willing to pay $25 per hour. Research the range of fees in your area. Some trainers list fees on their websites. Others will have to be contacted by phone. You can either be straightforward and say you are a new trainer in the area who is wondering what other trainers charge, or if you are more comfortable, pose as a dog owner inquiring about training services. If you are completely mortified at the thought of making these calls, solicit a friend to make the inquiries.

*What Type of Training?*

Once you have determined the average price range for your area, decide what type of training you will offer. If you plan to focus on puppy training, basic obedience and mild behavior problems, your fees should fall within the normal range. If you plan to address complex behavior issues such as aggression or separation anxiety, your fees should be higher for those cases. After all, you will invest more time and effort on them than on your average training sessions. Not only will there be more time spent writing up notes and formulating protocols, but you are likely to spend more time consulting with clients by phone or e-mail between sessions. Aggression cases in particular merit higher rates due to the increased risk of personal injury and liability.

## You Want Me to go Where?

Next, consider the geographical area you will serve, so that you can take travel time into account. If a client lives fifteen minutes from your home, that translates to half an hour total travel time. If a client lives an hour away, two hours of your time will be spent traveling to and from the appointment! While you cannot expect clients to pay three times your normal hourly rate, you can certainly add "travel charges" when a client lives outside a pre-determined service area. One trainer I know charges a travel fee of one dollar per mile for anything over twenty miles one way from his home. For example, since his normal rate is $80 per hour, if the client lives 30 miles from his home, a one-hour session would cost $90.

How much you charge for travel time will depend on what the market will bear for your own area. Keep in mind that if your normal travel time between sessions is one hour, you will be able to do fewer appointments in a day than if your average travel time between sessions were twenty minutes. Charge accordingly to ensure that you make a sufficient income.

## What about "Freebie" Items?

If you intend to hand out booklets or other "freebie" items (other than handouts you have created), your fees should include the price of those items. No one wants to find out after the fact that a training session is going to cost more than initially quoted. If you plan to hand out two booklets on a regular basis, and those booklets cost you $2.00 apiece at bulk rate, add $5.00 to your training fee (this includes a $1.00 markup). It is better to raise your rates slightly and then "give away" items than to charge piecemeal for extras.

# Setting Fees Worksheet

## Average Rates of Local Trainers

Basic training:

$_____ to _____ per hour

$_____ to _____ for _____ sessions (packages)

Specialized training (aggression, complex behavior issues):

$_____ to _____ per hour for (type of training)_____

$_____ to _____ per hour for (type of training)_____

$_____ to _____ for _____ sessions (packages)

## Type of Training I will Offer

_____

_____

## My Rates

Basic Training:

Single sessions: $_____ per hour

Package deals:  $_____ for _____ sessions

Specialized Training (aggression, complex behavior issues):

Single sessions: $_____ per hour

Package deals:  $_____ for _____ sessions

**Standard Service Area** (No travel charge)

_____
(by distance or area)

## Travel Fees

Area _____ Travel fee $ _____

Area _____ Travel fee $ _____

Area _____ Travel fee $ _____

## "Giveaway" Items

Item _____ My Cost $_____ Add to fee $_____

Item _____ My Cost $_____ Add to fee $_____

Item _____ My Cost $_____ Add to fee $_____

Item _____ My Cost $_____ Add to fee $_____

## Items I will Sell to Clients

Item _____My Cost _____ Sales Price $ _____

Item _____My Cost _____ Sales Price $ _____

Item _____My Cost _____ Sales Price $ _____

Item _____My Cost _____ Sales Price $ _____

Item _____My Cost _____ Sales Price $ _____

Item _____My Cost _____ Sales Price $ _____

# 5

# Singles vs. Packages

Training sessions may be sold individually or in packages. If you choose to sell individual sessions, you will collect payment at each session, with no further obligation on your part or the client's to continue training. If you sell packages, you will collect a lump sum for a series of discounted sessions. There are pros and cons to each approach.

*She Sells Singles by the Seashore*

The first few years I did in-home training, I only sold single sessions. This was partly a marketing strategy, as most of the trainers in my area offered packages only—and large, expensive ones at that. When local dog owners called other ads in the phone book, they were told that training would cost anywhere from $600 to $1,000. When they called me, they were relieved to hear that they could proceed one session at a time and that the initial layout would be only $120 (1.5 hours at $80 per hour). I would, of course, give an honest estimate of how many sessions would be required in total.

Some people preferred the single sessions because they did not have funds available to purchase a package, or because the package fees simply sounded so much higher. It is ironic that many of those same people ended up doing as many single sessions with me as they would have in a discounted package—and they paid full price.

If a client needs only one lesson to solve a minor problem, I will not attempt to sell extra lessons. Housebreaking, for example, is normally a one-session deal. I am not promising that in one session the dog will never urinate in the house again, but that in one session the owner will have all the necessary information to follow through and resolve the issue. I know of trainers who, regardless of the dog's problem, attempt to sell owners a six- or eight-session package. While advising more sessions is fine if they are truly warranted, selling more sessions than necessary for the sole purpose of padding one's income is unethical. People appreciate honesty, and word of mouth builds reputations. I would rather have a client purchase one session and then refer me to two other people than to pay me for training that is not needed.

Another advantage to offering single sessions is that the "no commitment" benefit pertains not only to the client, but to the trainer as well. While the majority of my clients are pleasant people with lovely dogs, every now and then one comes along to make me thankful for the single-session approach. It isn't pretty, but it's true: sooner or later there will be a client you simply prefer not to see again anytime soon. (*"Can we schedule that next appointment for, say, when hell freezes over?"*) In those cases, the single session is your friend. It is easy enough to end a session by suggesting the person work on the exercises for a few weeks and then give you a call to schedule the next session. Hopefully that call will never come; and if it does, you can gracefully decline.

I can summarize the drawbacks of the single-session approach in one word: *cancellations!* Where there is no financial obligation, there is a much greater chance that clients will cancel appointments, sometimes at the last minute. To the average person who has had a busy week or had "something come up," it is no big deal to postpone or cancel a dog training appointment. However, it might be a big deal to *you*, especially if the appointment is cancelled at the last minute and you could have scheduled another in its place.

If you sell single sessions, you are also at the mercy of cancellations' relative, the no-show. A no-show means that you arrive at the client's home at the scheduled time and—*surprise!*—the person is nowhere to be found. A no-show can be terribly frustrating, particularly if you have raced to get to the appointment on time or traveled a long distance.

No-shows can even happen despite the fact that you have dutifully phoned the night before to confirm the appointment. After waiting fifteen minutes, you might feel like raising your leg and leaving your "calling card" on the client's door. Leave a note instead. Let the person know you were there for the appointment on time, how long you waited, that you hope everything is all right, and to please call to reschedule. In the meantime, unfortunately, you are out the training fee. If you mentioned a cancellation fee for no-shows when you spoke, you could send an invoice; but you might not be able to collect. As a contract has not been signed, it would cost you more time and money to take the client to small claims court than would be worthwhile.

*Packages: The Whole Enchilada*

There are various ways to structure training packages. Some trainers sell six or eight sessions and require the client to pay the entire fee up front. Others sell as many sessions, but allow the client to pay half up front and half at the halfway mark. Some trainers prefer to sell smaller packages of three or four sessions.

The type of training you do will determine in part what size packages you should sell. If you do mostly basic obedience training and aim to train multiple behaviors to the point of fluency (reliability regardless of environment or distractions) or close to it, you would do well to sell six- or eight-session packages. If you have clients whose dogs have mild behavior issues and could use a bit of basic obedience, you could offer packages of three to four sessions. It really comes down to the client's needs and level of commitment, along with your own preferences. You could always offer more than one type of package. That would afford you more opportunities to customize programs and to offer a wider range of affordability.

Although I only train dogs and owners together, some trainers offer packages where they work part of the time with the dog only. In this scenario, the trainer does a number of sessions with the dog (e.g., thirty minutes, three times per week) without the owner present. Trainer and owner meet periodically to review what was accomplished and to teach the owner how to continue to work with the dog.

Getting back to owner-present sessions: although I will sell a single session if one is truly all that is needed, if a few sessions are warranted, I offer a three-session package. However, I normally wait until the end of the first session to mention the deal. (The exception would be if I felt mentioning the package discount would make the difference in getting a caller to make an appointment.) Completing the session before making the offer allows me to better gauge how much work the dog needs and how many sessions it would take to teach the necessary skills to both dog and owner. It also allows the owner to see the training first-hand before making a commitment, and affords me the opportunity to decide whether I want to engage in further training sessions. (In those rare instances in which I do not wish to return, I simply do not offer the package.)

Based on my rate of $80 per hour, the first 1.5 hour session is $120 and the following two are $80 each. Therefore, three sessions would normally cost $280. Pre-paying this package, however, brings the price down to $250—a savings of $30. I have had very few people turn down the offer. After those sessions have been completed, if more sessions are warranted I will offer the choice of continuing one session at a time, or if appropriate, offer a (smaller) discount on three more pre-paid sessions.

Package deals are advantageous for clients and their dogs, as they maintain a high level of commitment to the training process. The best thing about selling packages? No cancellations! …Well, at least no last-minute cancellations, and those are the truly aggravating ones. People are much less likely to cancel an appointment for which they have pre-paid, especially if the contract stipulates forfeiture of that session if sufficient notice is not given (more on that in a minute). Another high point about selling packages is, of course, that lump-sum chunk of change in your bank account.

Ironically, I had a strange reaction when I first began offering packages. The client would pre-pay the package, which was great; but at the second and third sessions, it felt so strange not to get paid at the end of the lesson! I had become conditioned to receiving immediate reinforcement for my efforts. Eventually I got used to it, though, and can now look back and see how much my business has improved since I began offering packages.

*Let's Agree, Shall We?*

Whether you sell single sessions or packages, it is crucial to have your clients sign a contract. The agreement should cover liability issues, state fees, and stipulate what specifically is included in those fees. (See *Appendix A* for sample contracts.)

Package deal contracts should state that any cancellation of less than twenty-four hours notice, and any no-show, will be counted as one appointment. So if the client who has pre-paid three appointments calls you the morning of the second appointment to say she has not had time to work with the dog that week, that appointment is forfeited and she now has only one left.

You might feel awkward informing a client that she has forfeited an appointment, but stick to your guns. If you don't, you will lose money, as you could have taken another appointment in its place. That said, I am somewhat flexible on this policy. If a client calls the night before our appointment and says her child has just come down with the flu, or she was called in to work, I will reschedule without penalty. But it is good to have the clause in place so that you can make judgement calls.

A package deal contract should also set a time limit on the completion of training. It is reasonable to expect that two hour-long follow-up sessions be completed within a month of the date of the contract. If you do not stipulate a time frame, training can stretch out endlessly and lose momentum. You do not want to be obligated to a client who calls six months later to schedule that last appointment.

Bring your printed contract to a copy center and ask them to print it as a two-part form—white copy on top, yellow copy attached. Once clients have signed, leave them with the yellow copy. Your copy can either be attached to the client's information sheet, or kept in a separate contract folder at home.

There is no need to feel pressured to make a final decision on how to structure your services. You can certainly start out selling single sessions and then eventually, try out different package deals. You will soon get a feel for which structure works to your best advantage.

# Part III

# *Opportunity Knocks, but Business Calls!*

# 6

# *Top Ten Phone Intake Questions*

When a potential client calls, your goal is to gather pertinent information in a timely manner, while establishing rapport. If you do this successfully and your rates are perceived as affordable, more often than not, your conversation will result in the scheduling of an appointment.

Keep a pad or notebook near the phone so you can jot down information as you chat. This will come in especially handy if the caller needs to check with a spouse or think things over (translation: "call around some more") before committing to an appointment. Imagine this: Patsy, owner of Dexter the Destructo Doxie, calls back a week after your initial conversation. She says she has talked it over with her husband and would like to make an appointment. Imagine how Patsy might feel if you were to answer, "Uh, yes I think I remember talking to you… what kind of dog do you have and what was it about?" Referring to your notes, on the other hand, would allow you to answer brightly, "Oh yes, Patsy with Dexter the destructive Doxie!" Trust me, most days I couldn't tell you what I had for breakfast, but callers are thrilled that I "remember" details about them and their dogs.

The initial phone call is not the time for an in-depth interview, but the following questions should be asked:

*1. Do you live in the area?*

Even if you only advertise in your own town, ask early in the conversation where the caller lives. You never know how someone was referred, and the caller could live out of your service area. Despite the fact that my website clearly states the area I serve, because of the ease of browsing for services on the internet, I have actually received calls from other states! If you do not ask early on, you might waste valuable time gathering information on issues that will, in the end, be referred to another trainer.

## 2.  How were you referred?

Knowing how callers were referred will help you to decide where to continue to spend your advertising dollars. It can also help to point up areas in which referrals have been lacking, so you can investigate and hopefully remedy the situation.

If someone was referred by a veterinarian, there is already a certain level of buy-in. People trust their vets' judgement, so they are already more likely to make an appointment (and to comply with your suggestions during training). A referral from the phone book can alert you that the caller may be a comparison shopper, so it will be especially important to give her something other than just numbers to base her choice upon (more on that in the upcoming *Phone Scripts*).

Knowing how a caller was referred may also give you an idea of what to expect when she becomes a client. For example, when a caller tells me she was referred through adopting a dog from Rescue Group A, I know her dog was temperament-tested and matched as carefully with the new home as possible. On the other hand, when a caller tells me she was referred through adopting a dog from Rescue Group B, unfortunately, I know her dog might have some aggression issues.

## 3.  What is your dog's breed, age, gender and name?

Beyond simply noting this information for your records, in some cases these details can give you insight into a dog's issues. Since some behaviors are inherently stronger in certain breeds, it is important to know the dog's breed or breed group. For example, if the dog-aggressive dog is one of the bully-type breeds (e.g., American Staffordshire Terrier, American Pit Bull Terrier, American Bulldog), aggression toward other dogs would not be unusual. If it were a Golden Retriever, aggression toward other dogs would be much less common. It is possible that you would not get the bully breed dog as far along in accepting other dogs as you would the Golden Retriever.

Trainers should not be "breedist," but knowing the tendencies of various breeds is extremely helpful. Is the trash-raiding dog a Beagle? Not surprising, as scent-hounds can be easily distracted by scents in the environment. Knowing this, you would discuss managment with the Beagle owner, and might especially focus on training a strong attention response and swift, instant recalls. (For books on breed-specific characteristics, see *Appendix C*.)

The dog's age is important as well. If a caller says her eight-week-old puppy has a housebreaking problem, that is perfectly normal. But if a caller says the three-year-old indoor dog she has had from a pup is still urinating on the carpet, you know (assuming it is not a medical problem) there is probably a lack of follow-through on the owner's part. If a caller's dog is eight months old, some of the dog's issues might be related to the onset of adolescence; an older dog might have medical issues that are affecting his behavior.

Gender can come into play in dog-dog aggression and other behavior issues. For example, two females in a home are more likely to fight with each other than are male-female pairings; males are more likely to mark in the house than females. Medical issues can be gender-related as well, such as spay incontinence.

Lastly, ask for the dog's name. This might not offer much useful information—well, if they've named the dog Cujo it might tell you something about the owner—but referring to the dog by his name gives the conversation more of a warm, friendly tone than calling him "the dog" throughout the conversation.

## 4. Who else is living in the home?

This information can be vital. For example, an aggression issue can be particularly worrisome when there are young children in the home. (When you ask for the names of family members, be sure to ask for children's ages as well.) The presence of young children also makes reliable management more difficult; doors and gates may be left ajar, and parents have their hands full watching kids *and* dogs. In a home with a young son, the child might be interacting too roughly with the dog. Children in the home, combined with the nature and severity of the dog's issues, could make the difference as to whether you feel comfortable taking a case at all.

If an elderly person is living in the home, potential issues might involve the combination of thin skin and razor-sharp puppy teeth; a lack of physical coordination or strength; or memory-defect-related spotty management. The issue might not even involve a family member, but a live-in housekeeper, roomate or other resident. For now, simply asking who lives in the home is enough. During the history-taking process, you will get a better idea of how each person relates with the dog.

5.   *Are there other pets in the home?*

If there is another dog in the home, ask how the dogs get along. While the call might be about the newly rescued dog urinating on the carpet, if the two dogs are fighting, the new one might not be in the home long enough for house-soiling to be an issue. Also, ask about the second dog's reaction to strangers. Sometimes, because an owner is not focused on the second dog, she might not think to mention his pesky habit of biting unfamiliar people at the door!

The "other pets" question can also yield information about cat-chasing, lack of knowledge about introducing pets to each other, management issues and more.

6.   *What can I help you with today?*

Aaahh—the million-dollar question. Callers will often begin with one issue but then as you chat, realize there are others. Let the person talk, take notes, and ask questions. Try to get the caller to clarify the main issue about which she is calling. If she begins to ramble, or there are an excessive number of secondary issues involved, suggest she make a list so you can cover as many issues as possible at the session.

Although this is not the time to take a detailed history (that will be done at the session), there are pieces of the puzzle that should be in place before scheduling an appointment, or deciding whether you want to take the case. For example, Dan tells you that Diesel, his two-year-old male German Shepherd, is "a little nervous around new people." Should you simply jot down "nervous around new people" and move on? Absolutely not! Rather than accepting Dan's interpretation of Diesel's internal state, ask what Diesel specifically *does* when he meets an unfamiliar person. After all, Dan's idea of "nervous" could mean that Diesel hides behind him when they encounter people on walks; or it could mean that when unfamiliar people walk through the front door, Diesel greets them by bestowing multiple puncture wounds. This type of information falls squarely in the category of "Things that are Good to Know."

If you train long enough, you will eventually develop a sort of sixth sense about when callers are omitting an important bit of information. I have had calls where nothing whatsoever was mentioned about the dog being aggressive—but I had a nagging doubt, and upon persistent questioning, found that although the original complaint was unrelated, the dog did indeed have an aggression issue. If you are ever in doubt, or just "have a feeling," keeping asking questions. Once you have all the pertinent information, you can make an informed decision as to whether to schedule an appointment or pass on the case altogether.

7.  *How long has this been a problem?* and
8.  *Why are you seeking help now?*

These two questions can provide crucial information. The dog might have had a housebreaking problem for the last two years, but the couple is only calling for help now because they are getting new carpeting. This alerts you that if not for the new carpeting, they would have been unwilling to make a serious effort to solve the problem and may be lax about modifying other unwanted behaviors as well.

Or the scenario might be more serious: Jennifer calls you because Tiny, her two-year-old male terrier mix, is "a bit nippy with kids." Of course you will find out exactly what "a bit nippy" means, but asking why Jennifer is calling for help *now* can give you an equally important piece of the puzzle. The answer is, unfortunately, likely to involve a bite incident. It is a sad fact that many owners will not call a trainer until an incident alerts them that a behavior has gone from annoying to unacceptable. "Johnny had friends over last week and Tiny bit one of them," Jennifer might reply. Ah, now you have a whole different scenario than Tiny simply being "a bit nippy." Although the answer will not always be so dramatic, the information these two questions can yield makes them well worth asking.

9.  *Does the dog live indoors or outdoors?*

Ask this question, because many callers will not offer the information. If an owner says the dog is digging, barking and destroying the yard, knowing the dog lives outside 24/7 provides a crucial piece of the puzzle. Outdoor dogs are often under-exercised, under-stimulated, and possibly under-socialized as well—a potential red flag for your safety. Knowing that the dog lives in the back yard could also give you a clue about the family's attitude toward the dog (although this should not be assumed).

Even if it is your personal belief that no dog should live entirely outdoors, remain neutral and do not jump to conclusions. After all, the dog might be living outdoors because although the family is devoted to him, the son is allergic; so the family takes the dog on three walks a day and spends hours on end in the yard with him. Then again, further questioning might reveal that the dog lives in the yard because he is not regarded as part of the family, but as a guard dog who is now causing problems.

### 10. Has the dog ever bitten anyone?

Even if Betty has told you that Bitsy is a Toy Poodle whose worst offense is that she urinates on Persian rugs, ask this question. Often dog owners do not realize that for trainers, this bit of information is important. Oh sure, Bitsy might have bitten a person or two, but that's not why Betty is calling! After all, Bitsy is just a tiny thing and she didn't inflict any real damage. Notice that the question is phrased very specifically: "Has the dog ever bitten anyone?" It is important to phrase it exactly this way rather than simply asking whether the dog is "aggressive." As with Dan's interpretation of Diesel being "nervous," people's interpretations of what constitutes aggression vary widely. If the dog has bitten, be sure to ask specifically about the severity and circumstances of the bite(s).

Over the years, I have heard owners make all manner of excuses for their dogs. The dog isn't "aggressive," he's "nervous around people," "a little nippy," or just "mouths hard." (Maybe we should be politically correct and call these dogs "bite inhibition-impaired.") I had one caller who said the problem she was having with her two-year-old Pit Bull/Lab mix was that he was jumping on people. Upon careful questioning, it turned out the dog had indeed jumped on the gardener the previous week—and sunk his teeth into the man's arm! (Okay, on my planet we call that a *bite*.) But even when relating the incident, the woman insisted the dog was just "mouthy" and aggression was not an issue.

A corollary to this question is, "What does your dog do when an unfamiliar adult comes to the door?" Again, this is very specific. Hearing that a dog is "okay with people at the door" does not inspire as much confidence as, "She might lick you to death." If for any reason you have a gut feeling that more questioning is needed, ask specifically *what the dog did the last time an unfamiliar adult walked in the door* and how long ago that was. I have had conversations where an owner assured me the dog was fine with new people at the door, but upon further questioning, admitted that the two-year-old, newly confident dog had not greeted an unfamiliar person at the door in the last six months. You do not want to star in that "aha!" moment of discovering that the dog now bites strangers. Ask as many questions as necessary to get the full picture.

Once you and the caller have agreed to set an appointment, it is time to gather final information. Get contact information (including e-mail address), street address and if necessary, driving directions. Be sure to note all pertinent data you have received during the conversation so you will be prepared at the appointment. Include any comments the caller made that might be important, e.g., "We're sort of lax with him."

End the call by restating the date and time of the appointment. My wrap-up usually sounds something like, "Okay, Elaine, I've got you down for Tuesday the 26th at 10:30. It's okay to feed Bootsy early in the morning but please don't feed him for at least two hours before the appointment. Don't worry about having anything ready. I'll have everything with me that we need. I look forward to meeting you both!"

Nervous about handling callers? Practicing can improve your skills. Have a friend play the caller. Once you have ended the conversation, review the list of questions to see if any were omitted. Ask for constructive feedback. This exercise will also help you to settle into a comfortable rhythm of acquiring essential information in a timely manner.

---

### Phone Intake Questions

1. Do you live in the area?
2. How were you referred?
3. What is your dog's breed, age, gender and name?
4. Who else is living in the home?
5. Are there other pets in the home?
6. What can I help you with today?
7. How long has this been a problem?
8. Why are you seeking help now?
9. Does the dog live indoors or outdoors?
10. Has the dog ever bitten anyone?

7

# Scheduling Considerations

You might be thinking, *What is there to scheduling a session? You just set it wherever you have an opening!* Actually, there are a few things to consider. The following considerations are aimed at making scheduling efficient and sessions run smoothly.

*Must the whole family be present?*

In a case that involves any type of aggression, the entire family should be present (with the possible exception of very young children), as it is crucial to get as much information as possible about the situation. Sometimes the person who did not think it necessary to be there is the one who provides the key piece of information that helps to solve the problem. You might discover that Sparky's lunging at people on walks is exacerbated by the way Mom tightens up on the leash as people approach; or that Bruno's aggression toward the kids stems from the overly rough way they play with him. Having the children present is also helpful because kids often blurt out information that parents might have withheld. (Kids really *do* say the darndest things—and trainers love it!)

In a case that does not involve serious behavior issues, it is not necessary to have every family member present. Sure, it would be nice to have all parties hear the information first-hand from you. But nowadays with work schedules and the social obligations of adults *and* children, it can be difficult to find a time when everyone is at home. If you work evenings and weekends, finding client "family time" might be easier. If you must do your appointment with only one family member present, be sure she takes notes, masters the exercises during the session and is left with handouts to share with the rest of the family.

*Won't kids be a distraction?*

Whether children should be in attendance depends on their ages and on the nature of the dog's issues. If the kids are seven and nine years old and the problem involves the dog nipping and knocking them down, those kids should be present. Besides, it is often helpful for children to hear advice directly from "the teacher" rather than second-hand from parents. Teaching kids directly also eliminates the potential problem of misinterpreted or erroneous information being passed down the line.

Having kids present also affords the opportunity to give feedback and reinforcement. For example, if you wanted a child to "be a tree" when the dog chases her, you would model the behavior first and then ask her to try it. If she did not tuck her hands under folded arms, you would modify her position and then praise her for doing it correctly. Asking her mother to pass the information along might not yield the same results.

I do not have to tell those of you with kids that young children have a hard time sitting still for long periods. Do not expect that your client's four-year-old is going to sit patiently as you review ninety minutes of material, whether it includes actual training or not. Try to set your initial appointment at a time when very young children are napping or in school. Subsequent appointments, which are of shorter duration and involve more actual training, can be scheduled either with kids at home but occupied or, if appropriate, with the kids involved in the training. (See *It's Not the Dogs, It's the People!* for ways to involve children in training.)

*Is the time of day important?*

Depending on the behavior you plan to focus on, time of day could be a consideration. For example, if you plan to work on recalls, you'll want the dog active and alert. Knowing that most dogs have energy peaks in the morning and early evening and are more lethargic mid-afternoon, you would plan your session during the more active hours. On the other hand, if it is your first appointment with a young pup and there is to be more conversation and less training, scheduling the session during the pup's nap-time would work in your favor.

Take into account too the time of day *you* are most alert. Are you a morning person? I am—much to my husband's chagrin! So I try to schedule sessions that require my intellect and energy to be in top form, for the mornings. I will not schedule a complicated behavior appointment in the late afternoon, following three other sessions. Doing so would risk my being less than effective and possibly even careless. On the other hand, squeezing in a "new puppy" appointment after a few others would not pose a problem. Try not to schedule challenging appointments for those times you are not likely to be at your best. Assess your own physical and mental peaks and valleys and schedule accordingly.

*What about the weather?*

Temperature can definitely be a consideration. In the area in which I live, summers can be brutal. It is not unusual to have temperatures soar over 100 degrees by midday. I would not, therefore, schedule an appointment involving leash work at noon, but would aim for early morning or late afternoon. Not only am I heat-sensitive, but I would not want a dog burning paw-pads on asphalt, or a dog or client becoming overheated. Every climate has its own challenges. Some northwestern states have rain much of the year. You might not think twice about training in a downpour, but will your client or her dog mind? What about heat, cold or snow? If necessary, ask in advance whether your clients mind mildly challenging weather, and make sure their dogs can handle it as well. These precautions will lessen the chance of last-minute cancellations due to weather conditions. Know your climate and plan accordingly.

*Scheduling Tips:*

- Each time you enter an appointment on your calendar, note the area in which the client lives. When scheduling other appointments, try to group them together by area in order to minimize travel time and gas expenditure.

- If a client purchases a package of sessions, ask whether she would like to schedule the next few sessions in advance. If you wait until the next appointment to schedule the following one, the desired date might be unavailable—especially if you tend to get booked a week or two in advance. Scheduling ahead can prevent a loss of momentum in training and a loss of client commitment to working with the dog between sessions.

- When scheduling an appointment after a client's work day, try to leave at least a thirty-minute window before your arrival. If you are scheduled to train just as the client arrives home from work, things can go awry. First, the client could be delayed because of work or traffic. Second, no one wants to jump right into training when she is feeling rushed or stressed. And third, the dog might be too wound up from being home alone all day to focus. By giving dogs and clients at least thirty minutes to settle in, you will set everyone up to succeed.

-   Do not over-extend yourself by scheduling more sessions in a day than you can physically, mentally and emotionally handle. Years ago, I taught two Saturday morning group classes back to back, followed by private appointments—sometimes four in a row. It was great financially, but I was exhausted. There is a tendency when building your business to be so overjoyed to have clients that you cram in as many as possible, and bend over backward to accommodate their schedules. You will take appointments on days you normally spend with your family, and squeeze in a 7:00 p.m. appointment even though you have three sessions before that and evenings are not your best time of day.

    While it is normal to be more flexible at first because you do not want to chance losing clients, establish good habits from the beginning. Know your limitations and stick to them. I know trainers who are perfectly happy doing five or even six hour-long training sessions in a day. Four is my personal limit, particularly if a few are new clients and therefore longer appointments. If there are serious behavior issues involved, I will schedule only three appointments that day. Respecting your limitations will help to prevent burnout.

-   Leave yourself enough time between sessions so you are not constantly rushed. That might seem like common sense, but it took me a long time to get that one right. I would do three or four appointments in a row with only travel time in-between. I neglected to leave myself enough time to grab a quick lunch, put gas in the car or simply sit and organize my thoughts before the next session. Give yourself an extra fifteen-minute buffer between appointments. That way, should you get stuck in traffic or some other unforeseen delay occur, your remaining appointments will not be backed up and you will not be stressed out. On heavily scheduled days, try to leave yourself at least one longer break between sessions so you can rest, eat and regroup.

You might be thinking, *That's an awful lot of things to think about when setting an appointment!* Taking these considerations into account will soon become second-nature. Developing good scheduling habits now will serve you well as your business grows.

# *Phone Skills*

You might be an excellent trainer, but potential clients will never get the chance to benefit from your expertise if you do not have good phone skills. That initial call is your one brief chance to make a good impression and convince the client to schedule an appointment.

*The Early Bird Gets the Weim*

Maggie is mother to two teenage sons and Ghost, the Wild Weimeraner. With her hectic and often stressful schedule, she looks forward to having Ghost under control—the sooner the better. Before dashing off to work, Maggie left messages for three trainers, explaining that she would like Ghost to pay attention and learn some basic commands. Maggie returns home ten hours later to find that two of the three trainers have not yet returned her call. The last has left a message. Maggie returns the call, the conversation goes well, and an appointment is set.

The two trainers who did not return Maggie's call promptly might be good trainers, but they have less than stellar business skills. There are many otherwise excellent trainers who allow calls to pile up on the answering machine, sometimes for days. Many of those potential clients understandably find other trainers in the meantime. We all appreciate prompt, efficient customer service—providing it to your clients should be a priority. Make every attempt to return phone calls the day they are received. My personal goal is to return calls within four hours. If you have made the mistake of scheduling back-to-back appointments all day with no break, you might not have the chance to have full-length conversations with callers until the evening. In that case, take a moment between appointments to return calls. Explain that the call is important to you but you are between appointments and will call back later that evening.

If you find the prospect of returning calls during your training day overwhelming, leave information on your answering machine as to when calls will be returned. For example, "Your call will be returned within 24 hours," or "Your call will be returned between the house of five and eight p.m.." That way, callers know what to expect and you will not feel pressured during the day.

## Be Professional

I recently called a massage therapist whose advertisement I had seen in a local magazine. The ad was eye-catching and professional, and the therapist seemed qualified. I looked forward to booking an appointment with her. When I dialed the number, the phone was answered by an obviously annoyed, possibly drunk male who challenged, "Yeah?" For a moment I assumed I had dialed the wrong number. Still, I asked to speak with Susan. To my surprise he barked, "Hold on!" This was followed by a great bellow: "Suze! For you!" I hung up before Suze made it to the phone. Susan might have been a great massage therapist, but she lost a client that day due to an unprofessional business presentation.

Be professional. Answer calls with your business name, and if you prefer, your own name as well. For example, "Good morning, Canine Training" or "Canine Training, this is Janine, how may I help you?" Do not simply answer with "hello" or "hi," even if you are expecting a personal call. If you are overtired, not feeling well, or just plain don't feel like talking, let the machine pick up. While it is true that you chance callers hanging up when they reach a machine, you also chance losing the appointment and/or giving a poor impression if you chat with potential clients when you are not at your best.

## The Most Difficult of Notes: B Neutral

Remaining neutral while listening to callers can be difficult at times. I recently received a call from Leeza, who lived in a townhouse with her husband, Tom, and Doozie, their four-month-old Beagle pup. Doozie barked incessantly when he was left tied out on the small patio while Leeza was at work, so he wore an electric bark collar all day. Because Doozie was prone to nipping the two- and four-year-old children, he wore a muzzle any time he was indoors, unless he was eating or drinking. And he was never taken for walks, other than five-minute "potty" walks. Now, your reaction to this scenario is probably similar to mine. There were so many things wrong with this picture, I barely knew where to start. I felt sorry for the dog, and to be honest, a bit angry with the owners.

But regardless of how bad a situation might seem, it will not help to berate a caller. Sure, *we* know that Doozie's owners were likely making his existing problems worse and possibly causing new ones. But can we find something good in the situation? Leeza *did* make the effort to call a trainer, which said she cared about her dog and was open to suggestions. I told Leeza she had done the right thing by calling, as I could certainly help her to alleviate Doozie's problems and make everyone's lives easier. Had I said I thought it was cruel to set a young puppy up by leaving him tied outside alone and then punishing him for barking, I probably never would have gotten the chance to work with Leeza and thereby change the situation.

I did a few sessions with Tom and Leeza. As it turned out, the tying out/barking problem had started because Tom worked a night shift. When Leeza left for work in the mornings, she tied Doozie outside because she didn't want him in the house, getting into things and waking Tom. We got Doozie crate trained, and now he happily goes back to sleep in his crate indoors after Leeza leaves for work. Barking problem solved. Tom and Leeza now use tethers and leashes to help manage Doozie in the house when he cannot be supervised—no more muzzling. In the meantime, they are working on teaching him acceptable house manners.

As it turned out, Leeza had always wanted to take Doozie for walks, but he had pulled so hard on the leash that she did not feel physically capable. One head halter later, Doozie is getting two twenty-minute walks daily. The point is, by remaining neutral rather than being judgmental, you will often be able to improve the quality of life for dogs and their families considerably. So give people the benefit of the doubt, even if you initially feel the urge to strangle them!

Sometimes the call will not involve an unpleasant situation, but an unpleasant caller. Though it can be difficult, try not to judge the person or respond in kind. Some people are calling after a stressful day at work; others are embarrassed about asking for help; some are even being forced to call by another family member. There have been times I got to an appointment to find that the brusque caller I had not looked forward to meeting was actually a perfectly lovely person. To be fair, I doubt that any of us are pleasant on the phone 24/7, myself included. No matter how edgy or annoying a person sounds, as long as there is no actual verbal abuse, answer in a calm, pleasant, professional manner. This often has the effect of calming the caller, which in turn leads to an exchange of useful information and setting an appointment.

## Be Direct on What to Expect

Once you have ascertained the reason for the call and the severity of the dog's issues, it is time to relay pertinent information. Yes, this is the sales pitch, but it also gives the caller an idea of what to expect. Give a brief outline of how you work, the methods you use, and your pricing structure. For example: "Let me tell you a bit about how I work. I do in-home training, which means I come to your home. What I am really doing is training *you* to train your dog! In addition to my working with your dog, you will be working with your dog during and between sessions. The methods I use are gentle and humane, but are not permissive. This type of training is very effective and will actually be fun for you and your dog."

I have found over time that the bit about "training you to train your dog" is important. Early on, before I incorporated that piece of information into my standard speech, I ended up with a disappointed client. She had expected that I would come over and work with the dog, without her ever lifting a finger. Looking back, she had every right, since I had not explained otherwise. Now I am careful to let callers know that their participation in the training session and their working with the dog between sessions is vital. Also, explaining that "in-home training" means you are visiting the *caller's* home is important. Otherwise, some people assume that in-home training means they will be bringing their dog to you.

Let callers know what the first appointment will entail. For example, "The first session is an hour-and-a-half. I will sit down with you to get some basic information about you and your dog, and outline the main issues. Based on that information, we'll discuss ways to manage the situation so things improve immediately. We'll also discuss what training will be needed to accomplish your goals and how long that should take."

Let the client know ahead of time whether or not you plan to do any actual training at the first session. For serious behavior issues, an in-depth history should be taken before working with the dog. That can be time-consuming, so I am careful to let callers know that there will be less training and more discussion at the first session. Some trainers prefer that the first session be discussion only, regardless of the reason for the visit. If that is your preference, let the client know beforehand. While it is perfectly acceptable to simply take a history, formulate a protocol and set ground rules and management in place, if a client does not know what to expect, she could be displeased.

## "Seeing What the Dog Does"

I once did a session with a woman who lived in a condo with her human-aggressive Border Collie. I had instructed her to have the dog contained when I arrived, and gave a detailed explanation of what that meant and why it was so important. I had no wish to become Pincushion Number Six. I called when I was on my way to remind her once again to have the dog contained. She assured me that was no problem. As I strolled up the line of condos searching for her address, I noticed a woman standing in the middle of the narrow walkway with a leashed black and white mixed breed dog. When I got within six feet of them, the dog lunged at me. Although I jumped back just as the dog sprang, because the dog was on a retractable leash, he was able to bite me in the leg three times in rapid succession before I could move completely out of range. I was wearing thick jeans and the bites were minimal, but I was not a happy camper.

If you haven't guessed by now, the woman at the end of the leash was my client. When I asked what she had been thinking, her answer was, "I wanted you to see what he does." It is one thing for *you* to set up a safe situation so you can see what the dog does. It is quite another for a client to take matters into her own hands. Do yourself a favor; make it crystal clear that unless you specifically ask, you do not need to see "what the dog does."

## The Confirmation

Whenever you have training sessions scheduled for the following day, call those clients to confirm. The few minutes it takes to call and leave a message could prevent a wasted hour of your time, should the client have forgotten about the appointment. Confirming the day before also gives you the opportunity to remind clients about any instructions you have given, such as not feeding the dog right before the appointment. And, confirming appointments gives the impression of a professional, well-run business.

### Phone Skills

1. Return calls promptly, even if only to say you will call back later that night.

2. Be sure your live phone greeting sounds professional. When necessary, let the answering machine pick up calls.

3. Try to remain neutral regardless of what a caller says.

4. Explain what can be expected at the first session, and whether it will involve actual training.

5. Explain clearly that you do not need to see "what the dog does."

6. Confirm appointments the day before.

*9*

# *Phone Scripts*

I received an e-mail last year from a trainer who had read my book, *So You Want to be a Dog Trainer*. She commented that while she enjoyed it and appreciated the recommendations about such things as ending calls promptly and turning comparison shoppers into buyers, she couldn't quite make the leap to exactly *how* she was supposed to do those things. When surveyed, other trainers suggested that specific examples of what to say would be beneficial. Many said they would appreciate ideas on solving sticky situations such as how to end lengthy phone conversations in a manner that is firm yet does not offend, or how to deal with unpleasant callers.

Phone conversations can be uncomfortable for some trainers; after all, many got into the field in the first place because they wanted to work with dogs, not deal with people! But dealing with people is part of the business, and there are techniques that can help. You might find it helpful to tape some of your telephone conversations (assuming it is legal to do so in your state). As you replay them, assess whether you sounded rushed or impatient, asked the right questions, and kept the conversation on track. Or, using the following scripts as a starting point, have a friend play the part of the problem caller. You might feel a bit silly, but the practice will prepare you for the real thing.

On the following pages you will find descriptions of various problem callers, along with specific examples of how each could be handled. Over time, you will develop your own favorite techniques and phrases. Just remember, above all, to treat *all* callers with respect and regardless of the situation, to remain neutral and professional.

*Phone Script: Sociability Before Sales*

You might expect potential clients to ask a lot of questions about you. Surely they will want to know about your background, experience, and training technique. Right? ...Wrong. The average dog owner is usually concerned with three things: how much the training will cost; how long it will take; and when you can start. Unbelievable as it might sound, in all the years I have been training dogs, I can count on one hand the number of callers who asked extensively about my qualifications and training methods. It's a good thing parents don't choose tutors for their kids this way!

Many callers will ask first thing, point blank, how much it will cost to train the dog. Do not make the mistake of answering this question immediately! It is crucial to establish rapport before quoting rates. You do not, however, want the caller to feel you are ignoring the question. Following is a sample conversation that illustrates a graceful segue from a query about fees to establishing rapport, ending in scheduling an appointment.

C (Caller): *"Hi. How much does your training cost?"*

T (Trainer): *"Hi! This is Nicole. I'd be happy to give you that information. Let me ask a few quick questions so I can give you accurate pricing. By the way, what's your name?"*

C: *"Sylvia."*

T: *"Hi, Sylvia. May I ask what area you live in?"*

C: *"We're in Westfork, in the new tract of homes up on Peach Canyon."*

(I have established that Sylvia lives within the area I serve.)

T: *"I've been through Peach Canyon. What a beautiful area! So what kind of dog do you have?"*

(I have complimented Sylvia on her new neighborhood and segued quickly into information-gathering mode.)

C: *"A black Lab. His name is Rowdy."*

T: *(Laughs) "That's cute. And how old is Rowdy?"*

C: *(Laughs) "Well, my son named him. And he's really living up to his name! Rowdy is six months old."*

T: *"And what specifically can I help you with?"*

C: *"Well, Rowdy is really a sweet dog, we love him a lot but he's just out of control."*

T: *"Can you give me a specific example of what you mean by 'out of control'?"*

(Always ask for specifics. As previously stated, people have very different definitions of terms like "out of control," "nervous" and so forth.)

C: *"Well, he's fine with my older son but he nips at my five-year-old. He knocks him down sometimes, too. Oh, and he chews our shoes if we leave them out."*

(Rather than choosing this time to give Sylvia a lecture on management, I reassure her...)

T: *"Ah. That sounds like very typical puppy behavior. The good news is, it can definitely be improved. We can stop a lot of it right away with management techniques, and at the same time work on the training aspect so Rowdy learns what is and isn't acceptable. I can also show you some things your five-year-old can do when Rowdy nips that will help."*

C: *"That would be great. Also, Rowdy jumps on us and pretty much anyone who comes to the door. And he doesn't listen."*

T: *"Hmm. Again, pretty typical stuff, and all of these are behaviors that can definitely be modified. Does Rowdy know any basic obedience, like sit, down or come?"*

C: *"We've only had him a few weeks, but we taught him sit. He sort of knows come but he doesn't do it all the time."*

T: *"Great! We have a head start, since you've already started working with him. You said you've only had Rowdy a few weeks. Where did he come from?"*

C: *"We got him from the shelter."*

T: *"Good for you for adopting him. You know, Sylvia, Rowdy sounds like a perfectly normal, energetic pup who obviously has a great home with you. Now all he needs is some basic obedience and manners, and some ways to work off that puppy energy—"*

C: *"Yes, exactly!"*

T: *"By the way, Sylvia, how were you referred to me?"*

C: *"I got your number from our vet, Dr. Green."*

T: *"Great. Well, Sylvia, we can cover the basic puppy stuff at our first appointment, like nipping, chewing, and housebreaking, and I can show you some great chew toys that will really keep Rowdy's interest so he's not chewing on other things like the table leg—"*

C: *"—Oh, he does that too, he's chewing on our cabinets!"*

T: *"Again, very normal puppy behavior. I can also show you some ways to exercise Rowdy that you might not have thought of, which will get some of that wild energy out and help him to be more calm."*

C: *"Well, this sounds like exactly what we need. How soon can you come?!"* (Laughs)

T: (Laughs) *"Let me give you my pricing and tell you how I work, and then we can set up an appointment."*


The conversation up to this point would have taken approximately four minutes. I would have proceeded to give Sylvia my rates (including what type of payment I accept) and a rough estimate of how many sessions would be required. That would have been followed by setting an appointment, getting contact information and directions, and establishing that Rowdy is friendly with visitors. The entire call would have lasted no more than ten to fifteen minutes.

This sample conversation is absolutely typical of ones I have every day. What made the sale successful? Establishing rapport. Consider the subtle reinforcement Sylvia received throughout our conversation: she was complimented on her new neighborhood, congratulated on adopting a dog from the shelter, commended for already having started to work with him, and complimented on Rowdy's name. Sylvia was also assured that Rowdy's behavior was perfectly normal and could be successfully modified. By the end of the conversation, pricing went from being the most important factor to something that, assuming it was affordable, was not really a factor at all.

Contrast the rapport-first approach with answering the comparison shopper's price query by immediately answering, "Eighty dollars an hour." You would likely hear a brisk "thank you" and a sharp click. That caller would have no basis on which to compare your service to other training services except pricing, and the least expensive trainer would probably get the job.

I am one of the most expensive trainers in my area, yet I successfully make appointments with a large percentage of callers. Although it may help that they were referred by a veterinarian or satisfied client, phone skills still make a crucial difference. Regardless of what product or service you are selling, you are always selling *yourself* first and foremost. If people like you and all other factors are equal, they will choose your service every time.

*Phone Script: Keeping it Short and Sweet*

Dog owners love to chat about their dogs. That's fine up to a point, as it helps to establish rapport, which in turns enables you to sell your services. The trouble comes when you have finished gathering pertinent information and are ready to set an appointment, but the caller wants to keep right on chatting. This scenario is all too common, and if you do not master the skill of curtailing calls politely, you will find yourself wasting a lot of valuable time.

One trainer I know suggests keeping a remote doorbell near the phone to assist in emergency escapes: "Oh, I'm so sorry, someone is at the door, I really must run." (I have such a bad memory, I would probably never remember with whom I already used this ruse, which would eventually result in a suspicious caller commenting, "Boy you sure do get a lot of visitors!") Another trainer surreptitiously calls her home number from her cell phone so she can say, "Whoops, there's my other line. Sorry, have to run!" Short of these tricks, the easiest way to make a graceful verbal exit is to be polite yet firm. The goal is to let callers know that you find their comments interesting and important, but that further conversation would be better suited to an in-person exchange.

In the following example, I have been chatting with caller Marge long enough to ascertain that Bernie, her two-year-old Bernese Mountain Dog, has mild behavior issues and could use some obedience training. This exuberant boy knocks kids down like bowling pins, digs, has destroyed more than a few shoes and does not respond well to commands. At this point in the conversation, I have already asked the standard questions, established that there are no red flags, and am ready to set an appointment. Marge, however, is not done talking about Bernie. The call has lasted ten minutes so far.

M (Marge): *"—Oh, and guess what? The other day I came home and Bernie had chewed the remote! Can you believe that?!"*

T (Trainer): *"Actually, believe it or not, that's not uncommon. You know Marge, it sounds as though there are quite a few things we can begin to manage immediately so that Bernie's behavior improves. Why don't we go ahead and set up an appointment?"*

M: *"Oh! And also, my husband is getting very frustrated because if he leaves a beer can sitting on the coffee table, Bernie steals it and takes it outside."*

(By now Bernie and I could both use that beer.)

T: *"Again, Marge, these are things that can easily be managed so everyone will feel less stressed right away. Now, are you normally around on the weekdays or would a Saturday appointment be better for you?"*

(Since Marge did not respond to my initial request to set an appointment, I have posed a question that requires her to make a specific choice, thereby increasing the likelihood of my getting an answer.)

M: *"Well, I work during the week until seven, so it would have to be a Saturday. My son has soccer practice on Saturday mornings. Oh, that's another thing—sometimes when I bring Bernie with us to soccer practice he barks when the kids run by. And one time he—"*

T: *"—You know Marge, I appreciate that you have so much useful information to share. That will definitely help at our appointment. Since there are so many things to cover, why don't you make a list so that when I see you we can go over as much of it as possible. Okay—so if we set the appointment for 2:00 on Saturday, will that give you enough time to get home after your son's game?"*

(Yes, I did jump in and cut Marge off, but it was done in such a way that she knew I had heard her last comment. I then steered the conversation back to the task at hand and posed another question that required a concrete answer.)

M: *"Actually, 2:00 would be perfect."*

T: *"Great. Let me get a bit more information."*

(I would then quickly get Marge's address and other necessary information, and end the conversation with my usual wrap-up speech.)

A helpful technique when quoting rates to run-on callers is to quote your hourly rate *and* the rate for additional quarter-hour increments. For example, "Training is $80 per hour, and $20 for every 15 minutes after that." That way, should the session run over, your client will not be surprised when you charge for the extra time.

Did you feel uncomfortable even reading this script? Can't imagine yourself steering a conversation so firmly toward completion? Don't worry. This is another one of those things that gets easier as you gain experience. Even if you consider yourself completely unassertive, you will eventually become so exasperated at wasting time on prolonged calls that you will develop your own version of time-efficient call management.

*Phone Script: The Art of the Turndown*

The majority of calls you get will likely be from people with whom you would be happy to work. Of course, the dog might have an issue you are not comfortable addressing, such as severe aggression. In that case, turning the client down by referring the case to another trainer is easy enough, and is the right thing to do. Or it might be that the caller lives out of your area, or her work schedule does not coincide with your availability. Again, these cases can easily be referred to other trainers or gracefully declined with a simple explanation.

Then there are the callers who, because of their personality or something that is said, make you want to—let's just say, respectfully decline. As the conversation proceeds, you become more and more uncomfortable. While your lips are moving, your mind is focused on how you can gracefully extricate yourself from the conversation as quickly as possible. Ironically, unlike those clients you wish would stop rambling, this type of caller usually wants to get right down to making an appointment—the sooner the better!

If you feel your personality or training methods would clash with that of the caller, you could be direct and say so, and refer the person to another trainer. But there are bound to be some callers you would not only not want to work with yourself, but who you would not want to foist upon another trainer. Below is a sample conversation (based on an actual call I received), illustrating the fine art of extracting oneself from this type of situation politely.

C (Caller): *"Hi. I get that your training is gentle, but does it really work? I have a dog with some serious problems and I need a trainer that can get the job done, not just throw cookies at him."*

T: *"Why don't you tell me what the problem is, and I'll tell you whether it's something I can help with. By the way, what area do you live in?"*

(Although I sound neutral and pleasant, I already don't want to talk to this caller any longer than I have to, especially if he is not in the geographic area I serve.)

C: *"Bridgetown."*

(Darn. He's in my service area.)

*"Okay, look. Tank is a ninety-five pound Pit/Lab. He's not clipped, and he ain't gonna be. He's jumping the fence. Can you fix that?"*

(What have we learned so far? For one thing, Tank's owner is invested in his dog's "machismo" and is not likely to respond well to a suggestion of neutering—and yes, I meant the dog!)

T: *"Is Tank an outdoor dog, or does he spend time indoors as well?"*

C: *"We don't have dogs in the house. He lives outside. Last time he jumped the fence he almost got hit by a truck and my wife is freaking out. Can you help me or not?"*

(The idea of a dog living outdoors 24/7 makes me very uncomfortable, but I know I am not likely to change this man's mind. Tank could lose his life by jumping the fence and getting hit by a car; so, although I am not charmed by this caller's personality, at this point I am still willing to work with him for the sake of the dog.)

T: *"I can understand your wife being upset, and I'm sure you want to keep Tank safe, too. This sounds like more of a containment issue than a training problem, and is something I can definitely help you with. What's your name, by the way?"*

C: *"Stu. Oh and there's one other thing. Tank bit a guy last week that came into the yard. Well, it wasn't hardly more than a nip. I mean, the guy was kind of a wussy about it, if you ask me."*

(Ah. Now we have a whole different picture. This is not only a containment issue, but an aggression issue as well. It is not going to be a simple fix and will involve patience and commitment on the part of the owners. I want to know more before I decide whether to take the case.)

T: *"Can you tell me exactly what happened? Were you there?"*

C: *"No, I was at work and my wife was gone too. The water delivery guy let himself in like he always does. He knows Tank can get kind of ornery and I told him to just ignore it, but I guess this time Tank jumped up and snagged him on the arm."*

T: *"Do you know whether the bite broke the skin?"*

C: *"Like I said, the guy was a wuss. He was crying about going to see the doctor. He got these three tiny stitches. It was nothing. No big deal."*

T: *"Has Tank ever bitten anyone else?"*

C: *"No... he came close a couple times but he didn't get 'em... he's never out of the yard unless he jumps the fence or someone leaves the gate open, and no one comes in but the water guy."*

(Now we know a few things: one, it is likely that Tank is severely under-socialized—pointing toward possible fear-based aggression—and probably has some territorial issues as well. Two, Stu is not taking the problem very seriously, is not being responsible about keeping Tank contained, and probably would not be calling, had his wife not been so upset. Stu is, in my estimation, not likely to follow the type of protocol I would recommend for modifying Tank's behavior, or any other suggestions I might make. He simply wants the problem solved—yesterday. Still, I keep in mind that above all, we both would like to keep Tank safe and more people from getting hurt. So I throw out a suggestion to see whether anything short of a wave of my magic wand might work...)

T: *"You know, Stu, the biting issue could be handled entirely with management. Since you know the water guy's schedule, what if Tank were contained somewhere safely, like in a pen, on the days the guy comes? I can show you where and how to set one up."*

C: *"Look, I don't want my dog in a cage! Can't you teach him not to run away and not to jump on people and nip 'em?"*

T: *"I understand what you're looking for, Stu. You want the problem solved right away and for Tank not to bite anyone else, and I give you credit for being a responsible owner. But there's training and there's management. We can work with Tank on the aggression issues if you'd like, but he needs to be safely contained for now so there won't be any more bite incidents. And you know, the pen would also be a good safety measure until the fencing can be fixed, so he doesn't get out of the yard."*

(Stu, who is obviously frustrated, has now been complimented on being a responsible owner. Okay, folks, overall I do not consider him to be one; but at least he is trying to resolve this issue and I need us to be on the same team for the sake of the dog, not to mention the other people Tank might bite. Stu has received acknowledgement that his wanting the problem solved right away has been heard. He has been told that the underlying problem can be addressed, and that there is a fast fix for the immediate problem. That was my final bid. Now it's up to Stu.)

C: *(sighs) "You know, I'm not getting this. You're a trainer, right? If you're not going to train the dog, what are we talking about here?"*

At this point, I give up. I realize that Stu is not a person with whom I wish to work. He has unrealistic expectations and has spoken to me in a confrontational, exasperated tone that I do not care to hear in person. Besides, the training would never work, as Stu seems unwilling to consider even my most basic suggestions.

   More than likely, Tank will bite other people, working his way up to an extremely serious bite, after which he will probably be euthanized. Do I feel bad about this? Absolutely. In fact, it is the reason I spent so much time on the phone with Stu trying to find a common ground so we could work together. But it is obvious that working with Stu and Tank would not only be unpleasant, but would pose a major liability risk. I do not mean because of Tank potentially biting me, but because a lawsuit could be brought against the trainer of a biting dog, should he bite someone else after training has been completed. So now what? I'm still on the phone with Stu, I want out, but do not want to foist him upon another trainer, either.

T: *"You know, Stu, it sounds as though we're just not on the same page about what needs to be done to make this work. I think you might be better off with another trainer."*

C: *"Yeah. It sounds that way." (click)*

Regardless of how frustrated you get with a caller, or how unreasonable the person seems, remain polite. Even if the caller becomes rude, it will not help to answer in kind. Doing so might make you feel better, but it would not be conducive to ending the conversation politely and is guaranteed to make the person defensive. Instead, end the conversation quickly, keeping your tone neutral. The aforementioned, "I think you might be better off with another trainer" is one effective exit line. Another is, "You know, I'm going to pass on this. It just doesn't sound as though we would work well together." Neither of these lines place blame on the caller, and both offer a graceful exit.

Of course, you might not feel comfortable being so direct. If you prefer a less direct approach, you could say something like, "Oh, darn. I'm looking at my calendar and just realized that I'm completely booked for the next four weeks. I'm sure you don't want to wait that long. I can call you when things lighten up a bit, but I completely understand if you need to go with another trainer, since you need this solved right away."

Listen to your instincts. It is always a mistake to make an appointment if you are uncomfortable with a caller for any reason. Use one of the exit lines offered here or come up with one you feel more comfortable with, but do not allow yourself to be pressured. A few awkward moments on the phone now are better than hours or even weeks of frustration and unpleasantness down the line.

# 10

# *Things to Bring*

Regardless of whether your session will focus on basic obedience, behavior issues, or puppy problems, here are some basic items to take along:

1. *A notebook and pens (or other way to record information)* Even if you have an excellent memory, there is no way you will remember all the details of each training session. Every trainer has her own preferred method of recording information; mine is to use a 3-hole-punch notebook. Each client has an individual "client sheet" (see *Appendix A* for a sample) on which I record the information that was gathered during the initial phone conversation. I then use this page to take notes during the session and to record any follow-up information.

   One trainer I know brings along a laptop computer, types in pertinent data, then downloads it to her computer at home. This could be especially helpful if you deal with complex behavior cases, where note-taking is crucial. Alternately, behavior case notes could be recorded into a microrecorder and later transcribed. Whichever method you choose, be sure to note what was covered during the session, what recommendations were made, and what you plan to cover at the next session.

2. *Contracts* for package sessions were discussed in Chapter 5. But even if you do not plan to sell packages, you should always have your clients sign a liability contract. *It is imperative that you have an attorney review this contract.* Simply copying a contract from another trainer in another state does not ensure its legality in your state. (See *Appendix A* for single-session and package deal contracts that include liability clauses.)

3. *Handouts* are normally a single sheet of paper with pre-printed information regarding a specific topic. Given the low retention rate we humans have for information we hear, handouts provide a valuable backup. Even if a client took notes as you went along, those notes would still not be as comprehensive as a handout. Handouts can also address those topics that are important but that you prefer not to spend time discussing during a session. If you find yourself reviewing a particular subject often, create a handout.

---

### Ideas for Handout Topics

- *General Training Principles* (e.g., "Behavior that is rewarded is more likely to be repeated.") This sheet could also include instructions on where, when and how often to train.
- *Housebreaking/Crate Training*
- *Management*
- *Nutrition*
- *Health Concerns* (e.g., bloat, poisonous plants) Be sure to give general information only—do not give veterinary advice!
- *Leadership*
- *Recommended Reading/Viewing List*
- *Teaching the Recall* and other specific training exercises. If there are games you incorporate regularly to teach these exercises, include them, with specific instructions.
- *How to Stuff a Kong™*; why and how to use interactive food toys.

---

If you work with specialized behavior issues like resource guarding or separation anxiety, you could prepare handouts on those topics.

When I first started using handouts, I printed them on my computer as needed. Now I bring the master copy to a copy center and make 50-100 copies at a time. I keep files at home for each handout, and replenish the plastic accordion folder that I bring to appointments as needed. The accordion folder, with its sectioned pockets and labels, keeps the handouts organized and clean. (Accordion folders can be purchased at office supply stores.) *Appendix A* contains a few sample handouts. Feel free to use them as a starting point to create your own handouts, or if you prefer, use them in their entirety (with copyright notice intact).

4. *Booklets or pamphlets* In addition to my own handouts, there are a few publications I like to give clients. Those written by Dr. Patricia McConnell are among my favorites. Her booklets on leadership (*Leader of the Pack*) and on modifying behavior in fearful dogs (*The Cautious Canine*) are detailed yet concise, and are incredibly helpful. Dr. McConnell also has booklets on separation anxiety, working with aggressive dogs and more. (See *Resources.*) I order the two aforementioned booklets in bulk and simply add the price to my session rate so I can "give" them to clients.

   New puppy owners receive Gail Pivar and Leslie Nelson's *Taking Care of Puppy Business*. This dynamic duo has other booklets as well that make excellent client handouts. (These can also be ordered in bulk. See *Resources.*) There are many booklets and pamphlets available that would make great client educational materials. Peruse the Dogwise web site (www.dogwise.com) for the latest and best publications.

5. *Treats* (I am assuming here that you use treats for training. If not, skip this section—but I would urge you to reconsider the power that treats have to motivate your four-footed clients!) Do not count on clients to have treats on hand, especially at the first session. Even if they do have something the dog likes, the treats may be inappropriate for training. Training treats should be small and easily chewable; every trainer has a personal preference. I like Natural Balance Dog Food™ roll. This soft, sausage-shaped product can be sliced to any size, has healthy ingredients, and is carried by many pet supply stores. Some trainers prefer freeze-dried liver or other dry treats. I know one trainer who always brings along a small jar or two of baby food for hard-to-please dogs; another purchases cheese and fresh turkey breast at the local deli for all his training sessions. Lucky dogs!

   Whichever type of treat you use, always have an alternate choice or two handy. Even if most dogs like your usual treats, it is inevitable that a few will not. Also, some dogs are allergic to certain ingredients, such as corn or wheat flour. (Always ask about food allergies before beginning to train.)

If you have a few back-to-back sessions scheduled in a day, and you use perishable treats (such as the sausage-shaped food rolls), carry a small, insulated cooler with dry ice to keep treats fresh throughout the day.

6. *Leashes and collars*  Whatever type of training equipment you use, have it on hand to demonstrate proper fit and usage. The bag I carry in to appointments contains a flat buckle collar, martingale collar, head halters (one Gentle Leader™, one Halti™) and a leash, among other things. I keep a full assortment of sizes and colors of head halters and martingales in my vehicle, since I sell those items. It is one thing to inform a client that a head halter would benefit her dog, and recommend that she go out and purchase one. But it is infinitely more helpful to have a selection on hand so you can fit the dog with the proper size, demonstrate proper usage, and offer feedback as your client practices with the equipment. (Trying the equipment on the dog is also helpful because one tool cannot possibly be the right solution for every dog you encounter.) Carrying these supplies is not only a convenience for your clients, but is a nice way to supplement your income. (See *Resources* for bulk ordering information.) Although I do not normally sell leashes or flat buckle collars, I keep a few on hand in case a client does not have one or does not use the type with which I prefer to train (e.g., some clients only own a retractable leash). Lastly, I always have long-lines on hand for distance work. Of course, you could stock all of these items for sale to your clients.

7. *Other training equipment*  Any training tool you use on a regular basis should be easily accessible during appointments. If you do clicker training, for example, carry a supply of clickers, especially if you hand them out to clients. (I do not use clicker training for everything but when I do use it, I leave the client with a clicker imprinted with my business information—see *Resources.*)

If you are doing specialized behavior work, carry appropriate equipment. For example, if you do aggression work, you might carry an Assess-a-Hand, a fake plastic hand designed to save your own skin when testing for resource guarding and working with other aggression issues. (The Assess-a-Hand is discussed in detail in *So You Want to be a Dog Trainer* and is listed in the *Resources* section of this book.) You might also carry an assortment of muzzles and tethers (more on tethers in a moment). If there are herbal or other natural remedies you recommend to assist in modifying behavior issues, have samples on hand to show to clients.

8. *Interactive food toys/chew bones/toys* Trainers know that providing mental stimulation is half the battle when trying to get an energetic dog calm enough to focus on training. It is important that clients are aware of this concept as well. Recommend and explain the importance of interactive food toys, chew bones and toys.

   It is much easier to bring a small selection of items to show clients than to try to describe each one. Many owners are not familiar with even the most popular interactive food toy, the Kong™. This hard rubber, snowman-shaped ball has a small hole at the top and a large hole at the bottom, and is meant to be stuffed full of food to be excavated by dogs. I always take one along in size Extra Large, and stuff the small hole with a chewy treat so the dog has something to do while the owner and I chat. That way the client can see first-hand how effective this chew toy can be. (Normally the entire cavity would be stuffed, but stuffing the small hole of the XL size is quick and easy and works well, even for small dogs.) I had one client who, as she watched her four-month-old terrier mix work at the treat for twenty minutes, exclaimed, "It's like a puppy pacifier!" I absolutely agree, and now use that phrase when recommending the product to clients with puppies.

   If you recommend specific types of chew bones, e.g., bully sticks (aka pizzle sticks), take one along to show the client what it looks like. That way you can also be sure the dog is interested in the item before the client spends money on it. If there are common chew products you warn clients away from (e.g., rawhide), take a sample along.

   If there are tug, fetch, or other toys you recommend, bring a sample, show clients how to use them, and tell them where the items may be purchased. (This is also a good way to build a relationship with your local pet supply store.) You could stock these items for sale as well.

9. *Tethers* Although most owners are familiar with the long, steel-coated cables that are meant for tethering a dog outdoors, few have considered using shorter (three to six foot) tethers indoors. Tethers are an incredibly helpful indoor management tool. They can restrict the

freedom of young pups not yet housebroken, and adolescent and adult dogs still leaving a path of destruction in their wake. Until a dog is better trained, a tether can restrain him from jumping on guests. It can also help ease the transition of an outdoor dog to one who is allowed to spend time indoors, and be used as a safety measure when working with behavior issues such as resource guarding.

Since shorter coated steel cable tethers with clips can be difficult to find in stores, I stock them for my clients. If you are handy, you can make them yourself with parts from the local hardware store. (The end product should look like a leash with a very small loop at one end and a clip at the other.) You will need a machine to crimp the ferrules—those metal clamps that hold the wire loops in place—or have the hardware store do it for you. If you are too busy to spend time making tethers (or are just plain lazy like me), mail order them. (See *Resources.*)

10. *Taste deterrents* There are a variety of sprays meant to keep dogs from gnawing on things they shouldn't, the most common of which is Bitter Apple™. However, there are a small percentage of dogs who actually *like* the acrid taste of this product. (I should know—I live with one.) Since you do not want to recommend a product that clients might find ineffective, carry a few brands with you. That way you can spray a bit of the product on the dog's favorite off-limits chew item, and let the dog lick away. The goal is to get that "yech!" reaction, where the dog shakes his head and repeatedly lick his lips (or at least stops showing interest in the item). If one type of spray does not work, try others. I usually carry four or five different brands. My next favorite after Bitter Apple™ is called Fooey!™. Trust me, it really lives up to its name! (Remember to wash hands well after each session or you might find out the hard way, like I did, how awful these products really taste. ) Once the dog displays the desired reaction I announce, "We have a winner!" and recommend the client go purchase the product.

11. *Appointment book and business cards* Your appointment book should always be easily accessible, to schedule further sessions. The end of a session is also the time to hand over a few business cards. (Hopefully the extras will be passed along to others.) I usually hand mine over when the client asks to whom to make the check payable. Along with the cards, I present a refrigerator magnet imprinted with my contact

information, so clients can easily locate my number to pass along to others or to call with questions. The design I chose is cute and colorful, depicting a Cocker Spaniel sitting in a boot. Clients always comment on how adorable these magnets are! (See *Resources.*) If you have other promotional items, keep them stocked so you can hand them out at the end of the first session.

It is also a good idea to carry the business cards of (or at least contact information for) anyone you normally refer clients to, such as pet sitters or groomers. One more item to keep on hand is extra brochures. You might want to give one to a client to pass along to a friend, since it is more descriptive of your services than a business card. Keeping a supply of brochures in your vehicle will ensure that they are always available for restocking vets' offices and other businesses.

12. *Miscellaneous* Breath mints—I keep them in my training bag and in my vehicle and always pop one right before an appointment. Speaking of popping things in your mouth, if you are scheduled for a long day, take lunch or snacks in a cooler; you might not get the chance to stop or even drive through, and it is important to keep up your energy level. You might want to keep a change of clothing in your vehicle as well, in case one of your four-footed clients is sporting that oh-so-lovely combination of mud and enthusiasm. Although showing up for your next appointment covered in dirty paw prints might be understandable, it does not look professional. You might also want to keep hand sanitizer and a first aid kit in your vehicle, and doggie waste bags on your person in case your clients do not have them handy.

Although it might sound as though you would need a giant tote bag to carry all these items, they actually fit into a fairly compact space. I carry a bone-shaped, medium-sized nylon zip-up bag with a shoulder strap. It can accommodate most of the aforementioned items. (I had to buy five boxes of dog cookies at a trade show to get the darn thing!) The items suggested here are just a starting point. As you go along, you will add new products to your in-home "toolbox" and discard others. Networking with other trainers about what they take along is also helpful.

## *11*

# *Just a Word Before You Go... Safety*

In *It's Not the Dogs, It's the People!* I related the story of a very strange training appointment with a client who lived in a remote area of the desert. While nothing terrible happened, the encounter served as a wake-up call as to exactly how vulnerable trainers are when going into the homes of strangers. While male dog trainers might not be as much at risk as women, and most clients really do only want their dogs trained, it makes sense for every trainer to take a few minutes' effort to ensure their safety.

Safety Tips:

1. If you get an unsettled feeling when speaking to a potential client on the phone, even if there is no specific reason you can identify, *trust your instincts*. Do not take the appointment. Tell the person you are booked; say your fee is $500 per hour; or say your spaceship is leaving and you have to be on it. It doesn't matter what you say—just extricate yourself from the call and from making the appointment. I highly recommend reading Gavin de Becker's excellent book, *The Gift of Fear*. It discusses the value of trusting your instincts and illustrates the point with examples you won't soon forget.

2. Let someone know where you will be. Honestly, I do not do this for every new client. But if it is a single male client I have not seen before, I will leave my husband his name, address and phone number(s), along with the appointment time.

3. Bring along a cell phone and make sure it is charged. *Carry it in to the appointment*—it will do you no good sitting out in the car! Be sure to have a button pre-programmed to speed-dial 911.

4. Avoid confrontation. If you find yourself feeling uncomfortable at a session for any reason, do not argue or otherwise antagonize the person. Either finish the appointment and set the next if necessary (you will of course call and cancel it) or make an excuse as to why you have to suddenly leave. Say that you are not feeling well; that the pager in your pocket went off and you are urgently needed; or that you need to get a leash or some other piece of equipment from your car. Then drive away. Don't worry about being socially awkward. Do what it takes to stay safe.

Now that we've gotten *that* out of the way, on to the session!

# Part IV

## *Solving the Mystery:*

## *Taking a History*

# 12

# Taking a History: Or, "Pulling Teeth with a Smile on Your Face"

Arrive for your appointment promptly, dressed appropriately. Clean jeans and a t-shirt are fine; a golf shirt emblazoned with your company's name and logo is better. Closed, rubber-soled shoes are a must! If necessary, tie long hair back. Forego perfume and dangling jewelry. Wear a watch, preferably one with a timer that you can set for a few minutes before the end of the session. And be sure the equipment bag you carry has a zipper or other secure closure so dogs can't nose their way into it.

Your first task after exchanging pleasantries is to get basic information about the dog. Knowing where he sleeps, what and when he eats, how much exercise he gets, and other basics will paint a picture of the dog's lifestyle and allow you to make appropriate suggestions. Knowing what training he has had so far and what type of help he needs will allow you to design a customized protocol. When working with complex behavior issues, taking an in-depth, accurate history is crucial. Because the way you take a history can make the difference between missing a piece of the puzzle and solving the dog's problems, this entire section is devoted to the history-taking process.

To take an effective history, both you and the client should be relaxed and able to focus. Eliminate distractions as much as possible by asking your client to turn off televisions and radios, and to ensure that young children have an activity to keep them engaged. If the dog's presence is too distracting, ask the client to put him outside or in another room with a chew bone to keep him occupied. If you have brought along a Kong ™ or other chew item, offer it for that purpose. Suggest the client have paper and pen handy, since you will be covering a lot of information. If you can supply paper and/or a pen with your company logo on it, even better.

Sit wherever you and your client are comfortable. I prefer the kitchen, not only because the table provides a convenient surface for notebooks and handouts, but because most dogs have a good association with the kitchen. This can be especially helpful when meeting an aggressive dog.

## Conversus Interruptus

Try not to rush the interview process. If you have previously explained that the first session is mostly discussion, your client should not be impatiently waiting for you to begin training, and you should not feel pressured. Take as much time as necessary to obtain a detailed, complete history.

Be sure that when you pose a question, your client has enough time to respond thoroughly. Many of us have an unfortunate habit of interrupting others when they are speaking. Often the person says something that triggers a brilliant thought or question of our own; so we half-listen, just waiting impatiently to jump in and interject this gem. Try not to do this with clients. Simply jot down any pressing questions or thoughts so you can pay attention as the person speaks, then proceed when appropriate.

## Red Flagging

During the information-gathering phase, a client might mention something casually that strikes you as potentially important. For example, you have just asked whether Talia, the six-year-old German Shepherd, has any medical problems. At first her owner, Ben, says no; then, almost as an afterthought, he adds that Talia has had mild hip dysplasia since she was a pup. He explains that the veterinarian had recommended keeping an eye on it, but no follow-up x-rays have been done. This little nugget of information is important! It could explain why, during a training exercise, Talia is reluctant to lie down in a particular position; it could well explain why Talia snapped at Ben when all he'd done was try to brush her hindquarters. Place a check mark or other notation next to any bit of information you feel is crucial, to flag it as something that warrants further exploration.

## Poker Face

Have you ever played poker? The best players wear a neutral expression, regardless of what is happening in the game. That expression will serve you well when taking a history. It is inevitable that you will hear information now and then that you find unpleasant, or even offensive. Try to remain neutral, or at least to appear so. For example, you have asked Bob what he has tried so far to solve Tigger's digging problem. Bob responds that he filled the last hole Tigger dug with water and held her head under until she panicked. He'd read about the method in a book and thought it seemed like a good idea. Instead of blurting, "But that's cruel!" it would better serve the interests of both dog and owner to bite your tongue and ask in a neutral tone, "How did that work out?" No doubt it did not work out well, or you wouldn't be there. Besides, maybe Bob really loves Tigger and was simply ignorant of the stress that would be caused by employing that particular method. By remaining neutral you retain the opportunity to be of help. Offend, whether verbally or by the expression on your face, and you chance losing compliance and possibly clients.

*The Eyes Have It*

Having the dog present during the history-taking process can be helpful. Sometimes the most crucial clues come not from what a client says, but from your observations of the dog's behavior, his interaction with you, and his interaction with the client and other family members. For example, if your client complains that her dog jumps on people, yet his paws are in her lap as she absent-mindedly strokes his head while making the complaint, you have a hint as to where the problem might lie. On a similar note, I had a client named Louise who informed me that her "poor little Bitsy" had separation anxiety. As I questioned Louise, the Bichon lay on the couch by her mistress' side. Louise never stopped petting or cooing to Bitsy during the entire ninety-minute session! It quickly became apparent that the dog was not the only one with a separation issue.

Take note of all canine-human interactions. If the client asks the dog to do something, does the dog respond immediately? Does the client give the same cue repeatedly, without waiting for the dog to respond? Does the dog show avoidance behaviors when the owner reaches toward him? Does the dog seem uncomfortable when you look at him? This is all useful information. Often what you see offers more valuable information than what you hear.

Now that you have a better idea of the *hows* of taking a history, what specific questions should you ask? That will, of course, depend on the dog's issues. The following chapters contain questionnaires that cover basic and not-so-basic issues. They have been broken down into categories for ease of use, along with explanations of what your clients' answers might mean. You will probably not ever ask *all* of these questions of one client. They are meant as a starting point, to allow you to pick and choose the ones that are appropriate to your particular case.

*Next stop, History Questionnaires!*

# The Questionnaires

## Questionnaire: Background

*Where did the dog come from?*

It is useful to know whether a dog came from a breeder, shelter, rescue group, pet store, private party, or was found as a stray. Sometimes a dog's place of origin can help to explain the issues the dog—and sometimes the human—is experiencing.

Pet Store Pups

Unfortunately, many pups that are sold in pet stores come from puppy mills. Puppy-milled dogs live in cramped, unhealthy conditions and are often sick at the point of purchase. Note whether the pup appears healthy and alert. Also, depending on how long he was in the store and the age at which he was purchased, the pup might not have received much socialization or mental/physical stimulation. Some puppies remain in pet stores for months. That scenario could potentially produce a pup who is fearful of new situations, people or dogs, and whose problem-solving skills are under-developed.

A pup's having been purchased from a pet store could explain why a client is having a difficult time with crate training. The pup was probably kept in a small, glassed-in area where it was forced to soil in its own living quarters. Since crate training is based on a dog's instinct *not* to do so, and this pup has lost that instinct, crate training would not be the best method for housebreaking this particular pup.

Breeders

Like every other profession, there are good and bad breeders. Good ones breed for sound temperament and test for diseases that are prevalent in the breed. They socialize pups very early to new people, places and things, and begin teaching housebreaking and good manners before the pup goes to his new home. Do not assume the breeder of your client's dog did any of those things, unless you or the client have knowledge of the breeder's practices. It is helpful to ask where the breeder kept the pups (i.e., in the house or outdoors in a pen), whether there is any documentation as to testing for hip dysplasia or other diseases, and how many rounds of vaccinations the pup has received. (For information on OFA testing visit the Orthopedic Foundation for Animals' website at www.offa.org.)

All breeders have their own beliefs and preferences as to how their particular breed should be cared for and trained. Conscientious breeders pass those preferences along to buyers. A responsible breeder wants the new owner to continue feeding the same type of food, training the pup in the same way, and so forth. This can be a good thing or not, depending on the instructions that are passed along. Some breeders are extremely knowledgeable and dispense sound, helpful advice. I have, upon reviewing paperwork given to my clients by breeders, been very impressed by the quality and extent of the information.

Unfortunately, that is not always the case, and sometimes a breeder's well-meaning advice is not what is best for the dog. That puts you in the position of having to disagree with the breeder. When you ask what brand of food the dog eats, for example, you might find that the owner is feeding a low-quality brand because it was recommended by the breeder. Because the owner might feel a certain loyalty to the breeder, it is especially important that you explain in a neutral tone, without being derogatory, why the food is of poor quality. Then offer a better recommendation.

Over the years, I have heard some bizarre training advice that came from breeders, much of it steeped in old-school methods. I remember one particular gem of wisdom that came from a man who bred wolf hybrids (not the perfect pet for most people in the first place). He advised new owners that if the pup nipped, to nip the pup right back—hard—on the nose! I would hate to think how many people got hurt following that advice. The important thing to remember is that *you* are the professional, the one the owner is paying for advice—so don't be afraid to politely but firmly disagree with information that has already been given.

Shelters and Rescue Groups

Ask whether the shelter or rescue group from which your client adopted had any solid information about the dog. If the dog was found on the streets or spent time in a shelter, he might have fought with other dogs for access to food. In those cases, the dog could have developed resource-guarding issues. If the shelter was a cramped, stressful experience, the dog might also have developed aggression issues toward other dogs, even if he did not have them previously. Careful attention should be paid to the dog's physical condition as well. Of course, many wonderful, well-adjusted dogs come from shelters or were found stray and have none of these issues. These are simply things to keep in mind.

Many rescue groups have volunteers who take dogs into their own homes until a permanent home can be found. If your client's dog was fostered before adoption, the volunteer might have shared helpful information with your client. Perhaps your client knows whether there were other dogs in the home and how the dogs got along, and whether there were children in the home. Information about how the dog got along with the kids and how comfortable he was when meeting strangers would also be useful.

Note that the question is whether the shelter or rescue group had any *solid* information about the dog—meaning facts, as opposed to someone's subjective impression. There are shelters and rescue groups whose staff or volunteers are excellent evaluators of canine temperament. However, in many city and county shelters, lack of adequate staffing is a problem; employees have enough on their plates without doing temperament testing. While some shelters or rescues do valid testing, others may not have the staff or knowledge to do so properly. (How long the dog has been in the shelter at the time of the test, his physical condition, the testing environment, and others factors also come into play.) While temperament tests can help in weeding out truly aggressive dogs, keep in mind that sometimes a dog has appeared to be "social" or "safe around children" during the test when, in fact, he is not so in your client's home.

Pay attention to rescue/shelter assessments of temperament, but keep an open mind. If you are familiar with a particular rescue group, you might have an idea of the quality of their assessments. You might also have an inkling of the typical temperament of the dogs that group adopts to the public. Some rescue groups do an excellent job of testing and making good matches between dogs and potential owners; others, unfortunately, consistently place aggressive dogs in homes. Get familiar with the groups in your area so you know what to expect.

Something to watch for with dogs adopted from shelters or rescue groups is abandonment issues. Even if there is no background information on the dog, one thing we do know is that at some point, there was a separation of the dog from his home. Some unfortunate dogs bounce from one home to another, ending up in shelter after shelter as each new owner finds the separation issues (and resulting destruction, barking and other symptoms) overwhelming. Given time and patience, many rescued dogs acclimate beautifully to new environments. Do not *assume* when working with a dog who came from a shelter that there are separation issues, but keep it in mind and make suggestions accordingly. For example, if your clients have four days off to bond with their newly adopted shelter dog and plan to go back to work on day five, stress the importance of enforcing many short separations, working toward longer ones over that time period. (Actually, that advice applies to any newly adopted dog, but I especially stress the point to shelter adopters.)

Another potential issue regarding shelter dogs is that many people are drawn to rescue a fearful dog. And who could blame them? It is difficult not to feel sorry for the adorable fur-ball with the huge brown eyes, cringing at the back of the cage. While trainers certainly feel sympathy for these dogs, what we see looks more like a red flag signaling possible under-socialization and fear issues, including the potential for fear-based aggression. Often new owners are not aware that their new adoptee will require a lengthy behavior modification program. It is the trainer's responsibility to give a truthful prognosis of what will be involved in rehabilitating the dog.

Sometimes the dog's attitude is not so much the problem as is that of the owner. People who adopt fearful dogs sometimes make assumptions, the most common being that the dog was abused. Never accept "he was abused" at face value. "But he's afraid of men," your client protests. "A man must have abused him!" While that is certainly possible, the more likely explanation is that the dog was simply under-socialized. Dogs who are not exposed to many people early in life are much more likely to be afraid of men than of women and children. Men are larger, have deeper voices and move differently; it's that pesky testosterone. While fearful behavior often has its roots in under-socialization, trainers should keep in mind that the problem could have a genetic component as well.

So what difference does it make if your client assumes the dog was abused, or feels sorry for him? That person might coddle the dog. While it is wonderful to have saved a dog's life, and every dog should be given lots of love and affection, coddling a dog to the point of not enforcing rules and boundaries is not useful. A client who feels sorry for "the poor dog" is more likely to ignore small infractions and even behaviors which, without intervention, could escalate into serious issues. Sometimes the biggest problem you will encounter with a rescued dog is getting the *owner* to behave appropriately.

Private Party

If the dog has a known previous owner, ask why the dog was given up. Many dogs lose their homes when owners move, get divorced, or for other reasons that have nothing to do with the dog's behavior. Do not assume a dog has behavior problems just because he was rehomed. On the other hand, do not assume there are no issues just because the previous owner says so. I have seen cases where owners neglected to disclose everything from the dog not being housetrained, to having a serious illness, to biting unfamiliar people.

As you can see, the answers to the dog's point of origin question can yield useful information as to how to proceed with housebreaking, where the pup stands as far as socialization, and whether careful attention should be paid to the possibility of certain physical or behavioral issues.

*How long have you had the dog?*

Many owners do not realize that a dog who has been in a home for only a few days is likely to act differently than one who has been there for months. In rescue circles, there is what is commonly referred to as a "honeymoon period" when a dog enters a new home. This is the human equivalent of you being a guest at someone's home; the first few weeks you pick up your dirty clothes, help with the dishes and are careful not to cause a mess. But a few weeks later, there you are, sprawled on the couch with a bag of chips while dishes collect in the sink. Many newly adopted dogs are still unsure of their new surroundings and family and are on their best behavior. Chewing, destruction, barking and other issues might not surface for three to four weeks. Do not assume that just because the client says there is only one small problem right after bringing the dog home, that will be the case a month later.

On the other hand, some clients expect too much of a new dog too soon. A client of mine adopted a six-month-old pup from Lab Rescue.

She had raised her last dog from a pup and trained it without the assistance of a trainer. I had to give her credit; she was naturally very good with dogs. However, she expected this dog, who had been in her home less than a week, to get with the program and focus on her and respond the way her old dog did. She could not understand why the dog wouldn't down-stay like her old dog, remaining motionless as she moved out of sight. This well-meaning woman was simply expecting too much too soon. It is fine and even desirable to set rules and boundaries from the start, but it is important too to give a new dog time to adjust to his surroundings and to bond with his new family.

*Have you had previous dog experience?*

It is always helpful to ask about previous dog experience so you have a rough idea of the level of knowledge and experience of the owner. Some people have had dogs all their lives; that can be useful, since they are already familiar with the realities of living with dogs. On the other hand, that experience can be detrimental if the person has acquired habits that will have to be undone, such as feeding the dog from the dinner table or training in a harsh manner. Some owners have had dog experience, but this is their first puppy in a long time and they do not remember all that having a pup entailed. Most have forgotten it was so much work! Others have not had a dog since childhood. Take the owner's previous experience into account and proceed accordingly.

Very often owners of a new dog will remember their first dog as having been perfect. You are likely to hear comparisons, complete with descriptions of the near-angelic behavior of the first dog. (I think of this as PCPS, or Primary Canine Perfection Syndrome.) This is the time to gently remind owners that *this* is the dog they have now, and *this* dog's behavior is what needs attention. I often laughingly tell people that I believe the universe is set up so that the first dog is perfect—otherwise we might never get the second!

*Why did you choose this particular breed?*

You might find, when asking an owner why she chose a particular breed, that she has always owned that breed. The good news is that breed enthusiasts often have a fair amount of knowledge and experience with their breed's behavioral tendencies and medical issues. The bad news is, they may have unrealistic notions. Some owners are convinced that northern breeds are stubborn; others insist bully breeds need a heavy hand in training; some even believe their breed cannot be taught to eliminate outdoors! Refuting these myths gently but firmly will be one of your most important tasks when working with the breed-experienced.

You might find that the answer to the "why this particular breed" question yields other helpful information as well. For example, when Jenna is questioned as to why her family chose a Neapolitan Mastiff, she responds, "My husband likes the way they look." Uh-oh. Red flag! Neos are not Golden Retrievers, and while there is nothing wrong with appreciating the appearance of these large, handsome dogs, the breed has certain traits of which an owner should be aware. Neos are guard dogs and are protective by nature. They are normally wonderful with their own family members, but can be wary of strangers. In an environment where friends and relatives visit sporadically, especially where children are involved, a Neapolitan Mastiff would not be the best choice. However, since the dog is already in the home, you would stress the need for early and ongoing socialization and good leadership practices, especially as the dog passes through adolescence into adulthood. Without causing alarm, be honest about breed tendencies and do what you can to prevent potential problems.

*Why did you choose this particular dog?*

When I was a child, my parents adopted a puppy from a rescue center. I remember them telling me why they chose Skippy. The first time they laid eyes on her, my mother explained, Skippy was in the corner of a pen, defending a bowl of food from a snarling ring of dogs. My parents liked her feisty spirit. (I'm not sure naming her "Skippy" was a just reward for her bravery, but maybe that's just me.) Now, this could have gone either way. Skippy might have developed resource-guarding issues as a result of her daily interactions with those dogs. Fortunately, she turned out to be a well-adjusted, lovely dog who shared with everyone, including other dogs. But if you were a trainer whose client had just related the story of why Skippy was chosen, testing for resource-guarding might be on your to-do list.

Asking clients why they chose a particular dog can yield interesting and potentially useful information. The kind-hearted person who chose the fearful dog probably felt sorry for that dog. As previously mentioned, that could mean you will have to get past the owner's propensity for coddling the "poor dog." The person who chose the dog because of its

macho looks might be hesitant about getting the dog neutered, despite
the fact that it could potentially help the male dog-dog aggression issues
you are there to address. Although you will not always get such
specifically helpful information, this question is always worth asking.

## Questionnaire: Physical and Medical Issues

*Who is your veterinarian?*

It is a good practice to record the name of your clients' veterinarians, in
case there is ever a need to consult regarding the dog's behavior or medical
history, or to send progress reports. Sometimes an owner will be new to
the area and will not yet have a vet; if you know of a good one, make a
recommendation. Or owners might have purchased a puppy, but received
little or no information regarding health care. That offers the chance for
you to help expand their knowledge.

*Is the dog current on vaccinations?*

You might think this question would only be applicable in a group class,
but it is also relevant in private training. Ask how many rounds of
vaccinations puppies have received. Some owners are unaware at what
age pups are normally vaccinated, and some have not considered
vaccinations at all. Since parvo and distemper are potentially fatal,
educating owners about these diseases should be part of your initial puppy
session. Some veterinarians advise owners not to take puppies *anywhere*
until vaccinations are complete, at the age of four months. This is your
opportunity to discuss safe ways to socialize the pup, and the importance
of early socialization versus risk of illness.

When working with an adult dog in the home, asking whether the dog
is current on vaccinations is not as crucial. But knowing whether an adult
dog is current on the rabies vaccination is important when working with
a human-aggressive dog, especially if there have been known cases of
rabies in your area.

There has been much speculation in recent years about the possible
dangers of over-vaccination, primarily in terms of damage to the canine
immune system. Many vets now vaccinate every three years instead of
following the traditional annual protocol. Some owners forego

vaccinations altogether for adult dogs, instead monitoring titer levels (immunity levels measured by blood testing). While you should not dispense medical advice, if you are knowledgeable about these subjects you can mention them briefly, along with the suggestion that your clients research them further on their own as well as consulting their veterinarian.

*When was the dog's last veterinary exam?*

This question can yield useful information in certain circumstances. For example, when working with a dog who is reactive to touch, you might ask whether the dog can be handled without being muzzled by the veterinarian or vet techs. The owner might answer, "Yes, that's no problem." If you do not follow up by asking the approximate date of the dog's last vet visit, you might miss the fact that the dog has not actually been to the vet for some time. This is particularly important if the dog has not been seen by a vet since pre-adolescence, as a dog's confidence builds throughout adolescence and early adulthood; fearful cowering may have turned into fear-biting.

The date of the dog's last veterinary exam is especially important to know when working with any type of aggression, since some aggressive behavior has its roots in physical discomfort or illness. In those cases, ask not only for the date of the last vet exam, but which tests were performed and what the results showed.

*Does the dog have any known medical problems?*

Knowing that a dog has a medical problem can have a direct effect on your training. If a dog is diabetic, for example, you would not use training treats containing sugar. If a dog has an injured paw, you would postpone leash work until it healed.

A dog's medical issues can also offer insights about behavior. For example, your client tells you her dog has hip dysplasia. Flag that bit of information—it could explain why the dog will not or cannot perform certain training exercises. It could also explain an unwillingness to be groomed or handled in certain ways, or why the dog is reactive with other dogs. After all, a dog with tenderness in the hip area might not appreciate being jumped on by another dog, even in play mode.

Sometimes an owner will think a dog has suddenly "turned aggressive" when, in reality, the dog is in pain. A structural issue, whether in the hips, spine or neck, is something owners often miss, but you may notice as the dog moves. If you see something that could be a structural problem, call it to the owner's attention and suggest it be checked out with a veterinarian. A structural issue in the neck area would also alert you to be especially careful when considering your choice of training equipment.

While dog trainers are not expected to be as medically knowledgeable as veterinarians, you should have a good working knowledge of common canine medical issues. That way you can discuss them intelligently with clients and apply that knowledge to training and behavior. If you suspect something might be physically wrong but are not sure of specifics, ask whether the dog has had a recent blood workup or other diagnostic tests. If you suspect a specific illness, or know of a specific test that should be run, suggest the owner discuss it with a veterinarian.

If you have a good working relationship with a knowledgeable veterinarian or two, all the better. Consult them when you have questions about the possible connection between medical and behavioral issues. Ask what tests should be run and how the condition might affect the dog's behavior. The more well-rounded your medical knowledge, the more effective you can be.

*Is the dog on any type of medication?*

Be sure to ask not only whether the dog is on medication, but if so: what medication, for what reason, what dosage, and for how long. Certain medications have side effects of which you should be aware. For example, your client's dog has allergies and has been given prednisone; the dog has started urinating in the house. The owner considers this strange, since the dog is housebroken. Knowing that one side-effect of prednisone is increased thirst, you would explain the effect of increased water intake and the need for more frequent elimination opportunities. Certain drugs have a side effect of increased aggression in a small percentage of dogs. This is definitely in the category of Things that are Good to Know!

I had a client once whose dog was on clomipramine (Clomicalm) to treat separation anxiety. Upon further questioning, it turned out the person the dog had a "separation issue" from had moved out over a year ago! Do not assume your clients are aware of all the facts surrounding canine medications.

If you discover that a dog is on medication, research what the drug is used for and the potential side effects. While you are not expected to be a walking encyclopedia of canine medicine, you should become familiar with those medications that are most commonly prescribed.

*Is the dog spayed/neutered?*

This answer can tell you a lot about the owner's attitude, from the client who says, "Nah, we never fix our dogs" to the one who responds, "Oh yes, we're just waiting until he's six months old because that's what our vet recommends." Posing this question can offer the opportunity to educate owners who are not aware of the pros and cons of neutering, and if appropriate, those who might be planning to breed the dog. For example, the owners of an aggressive dog or one with a hereditary disease should be dissuaded from breeding that dog. Whether the dog is neutered can also supply crucial information with regard to certain aggression issues, such as male-to-male dog aggression.

*Does the dog have food allergies?*

You might be wondering why this question is important, as many trainers never ask about food allergies. There are a few good reasons to do so. For one thing, if your training involves the use of food treats, you do not want the dog to have an allergic reaction to the ingredients. Another reason is that the owner might unwittingly be feeding a food or treat that contains a common allergen such as corn. Allergies can make people cranky, and can affect canine health and behavior as well. If the client says the dog does not have food allergies but you suspect otherwise, suggest sources of educational information. If you have a handout to share on the subject, all the better.

## Questionnaire: Feeding, Treats and Chew Items

*What type of food is the dog being fed?*

You will want to know not only whether the dog eats dry food, canned or an alternate diet (e.g., a raw food diet), but what specific brands are being fed. Nutrition affects behavior, and it is important not only that *you* realize that, but that you explain the importance of this connection to your clients. By way of analogy, I often tell clients that when I drink five cups of coffee or eat too much sugar, I'm a whole different person! That usually elicits a chuckle and a knowing nod, and makes the point about the nutrition/behavior link.

Most owners feed dry kibble, either alone or with canned food. Unfortunately, some owners are completely unaware of the nutritional and behavioral effects of feeding a poor quality supermarket brand versus one with more healthful ingredients. Teach owners to read labels so they are not taken in by shrewd advertising. As I like to tell my female clients, if there were truth in advertising, none of us would have a single wrinkle! Explain that ingredients are listed on dog food bags in descending order by bulk weight. Point out which ingredients are healthy and which are not (discuss by-products, fillers, grades of meat), and explain how they can affect behavior. If you would like to expand your own knowledge on the subject, consider a subscription to *Whole Dog Journal* (see *Appendix C*), a monthly publication that runs excellent articles on the subject of canine nutrition and even compares brands.

If there are specific brands you recommend, explain why. If the products are hard to find, let clients know where they are available in their area. You will find that some clients feed a specific brand because it was recommended by their veterinarian. It is one thing for a food to have been prescribed for a specific medical condition, but if the vet recommends a brand of food you feel is less than adequate nutritionally, explain why you prefer other brands. (Never tell a client directly that you disagree with a veterinarian's advice unless a serious health issue is involved and you are absolutely certain the advice is wrong or could cause harm.) If you advise a change of food, instruct the client how to make the transition gradually so as to lessen the chance of gastrointestinal upset.

*What types of treats, cookies or chew items does the dog get, and how often?*

I had one client who answered this question with, "For treats, I give him those small Milky Way bars." Yikes! This is another one of those questions that offers the opportunity to educate. For example, while most dog owners realize that chocolate can be toxic to dogs, many are not aware that rawhide is also not the safest thing for dogs to chew. And why would they, when it is sold in most pet supply stores?

Some owners over-feed treats and cookies but do not make the connection with the dog being overweight or passing up meals. Then there are those who give their dogs a reasonable amount of treats but neglect to supply the dog with any chew items. This is your opportunity to explain that proper chew items (e.g., Kongs™, bully sticks) can relieve canine stress and are a great way to redirect all that energy that is currently focused on chewing the table leg. Explain the importance of avoiding canine "junk food" and make specific recommendations as to healthy treats and chew items.

*How many times a day is the dog fed?*

Free-feeding is discouraged by many trainers unless there are extenuating circumstances, such as a young pup being left alone all day (a whole other problem in itself). Why scheduled feedings rather than free-feeding? For one thing, scheduled feedings help to establish leadership. Food comes from the leader, not from that round thing that is always magically full. And if the owner is presenting the food twice daily, that means two daily opportunities to ask the dog to sit to earn something valuable. Scheduled feedings can also help with housebreaking; if you know when the food is going in, it is easier to predict when it is going to be excreted. And scheduled feedings can serve as a diagnostic tool; if a dog who normally eats right away turns his nose up at a meal, he could be ill.

If you recommend switching from free-feeding to scheduled feedings, explain exactly how to go about doing so, i.e., "Leave food down for ten to fifteen minutes, then pick it up and don't present it again until the next feeding." I am always careful to tell clients in advance not to feel they are being "mean" when taking away the uneaten food, that no dog will starve itself, and that most dogs catch on quickly and will soon eat when the food is presented.

*If feeding on a schedule, at what hours is the dog fed?*

Most owners who feed on a schedule offer food either once or twice daily. This information is especially pertinent when there is a housebreaking issue involved. A puppy who is fed at 10 p.m. and then placed in a crate overnight cannot be expected to "hold it" until morning. A puppy who is fed directly before an owner leaves for work will need a place to eliminate while the owner is gone. Explain the relationship between feeding schedules and housebreaking. I often suggest that owners who feed on a schedule keep a log of what times the dog defecates, so they can ensure that elimination opportunities are available at those times.

Changing the time the dog is fed can help to solve certain problems. For example, if an owner complains that her dog wakes her too early every morning, and the dog is being fed immediately upon her waking, simply delaying the feeding time by thirty minutes after she wakes can solve the problem. If a dog is left alone all day and fed as soon as the owner gets home, that dog has two reasons to be anxious: the owner's return is anticipated, as is the meal that accompanies that return. Again, a delay before feeding can help.

*Does the dog eat right away and finish the entire meal?*

You might be surprised at how many owners will say their dog is fed twice daily but, upon further questioning, reveal that the food is *presented* twice daily—but if left unfinished, remains available so the dog can pick at it for hours. That is not the same as scheduled feedings! Explain the difference.

Don't discount the value of the dog's appetite as a diagnostic tool. I often tell the story of how scheduled feedings saved Mojo's life. Mojo, my Malamute/German Shepherd/Rottweiler mix, has always wolfed down his food (along with anything else he could get his big, furry paws on). The day he walked away from a full dish of food, he did not pass Go, did not collect $200, but went straight to the vet's office. Although Mojo hadn't been *acting* sick, it turned out he was quite ill. In fact, that vet visit might have saved his life! Had I been free-feeding, I never would have been alerted that something was wrong. This story illustrates in a powerful, personal way the diagnostic value of scheduled feedings. If you have a similar story, tell it. If not, use Mojo as your example. I don't mind and neither does he.

*Where is the dog fed, and who is nearby when he eats?*

Some owners have been advised, either by word of mouth or in books, to feed their dogs in an isolated area, away from the family. As trainers know, this practice has the potential to lead to a dog feeling territorial over his food, the bowl, and even the feeding area. Explain that dogs should be fed in the kitchen or wherever it is convenient for the family, so long as the dog is not isolated. While it is best to encourage parents to teach children not to bother the dog while he is eating, get the dog used the children's presence at feeding time just in case. Practices such as having children approach to drop a bit of hot dog or cheese in the dog's dish as he eats will create a positive association with children approaching his food, and can prevent future problems. (Recommend this only if you feel the exercise would be safe, and only under supervision.)

If you are working with a multiple dog household, ask whether the dogs are fed at the same time, and where each dog is fed. This is an especially important point with working with aggression issues within the family pack. It can also be an opportunity to suggest that owners feed growing pups from separate bowls rather than the shared bowl they have been using, to prevent squabbles as the dogs mature.

*Who does the feeding?*

Food is an extremely valuable resource to dogs. As previously mentioned, providing this resource give humans leadership status in dogs' eyes. Of course, this simple act in and of itself is not enough to establish leadership, but in a situation where a specific person's status needs to be elevated (or the person needs to establish more of a bond with the dog), that person should handle feeding chores.

*Does the dog get "people food"?*

You might be surprised at the guilty look that passes between family members when this question is asked. There is nothing wrong per se with a dog getting certain types of "people food." In fact, food such as boiled chicken is healthier than the ingredients in many processed dog foods. While dogs should never be fed directly from the dinner table (unless one enjoys the sensation of eyes boring holes in one's back), there is nothing wrong with a dog getting bits of chicken or other bland, healthful "people food" well after dinner is over.

The other reason to ask about "people food" is that some owners are not aware that certain foods should never be fed to dogs. I know of one young couple who fed their dog a diet of mostly spaghetti with spicy sauce; I kid you not. Some people will answer this question with, "Oh no, we *never* give our dogs people food"—as though that were the worst thing a human could possibly do. In fact, many trainers use bits of cheese or hot dog as training treats. I ask clients, "If I held hot dogs in one hand and dog food in the other, do you really think your dog would be looking from one hand to the other thinking, *Hmm, people food...dog food. ...I* think not. The bottom line? "People food" is fine for dogs, so long as it is not harmful and is not offered directly from the dinner table or someone's plate.

## Questionnaire: Logistics

*Where does the dog sleep?*

Some trainers are adamant that dogs not be allowed to sleep on owners' beds. Others, myself included, find the practice perfectly acceptable so long as there are no problems involving housebreaking, destruction, or aggressive behavior. (A dog who gives the Elvis lip curl when asked to get off the bed has no business being up there in the first place!)

Knowing where the dog sleeps, in conjunction with other information, can provide clues about the dog-owner relationship. A dog who sleeps in the owner's bed is usually regarded as a close family member; one who is assigned to the garage or back yard at night might not be as much so (though this should not be assumed—further questioning would be in order). An answer of "anywhere he wants" is not necessarily bad, but does tell you management has not been a priority, which is important if the client's complaint includes housebreaking and/or destruction. The answer to this question might result in your recommending crating or tethering the dog (indoors) at night.

*Is the dog allowed on the furniture?*

As with the bed, some trainers believe a dog should never be allowed on furniture. My feeling is that if an owner enjoys cuddling with the dog on the couch, and the dog enjoys it as well, why not? Again, if there are aggression issues (e.g., the dog growls when requested to get off the couch), the dog should not be on the couch, bed or any other raised surface. Other than that, it is a question of owner preference. Owners can use furniture privileges as a way to increase their own status, by allowing the dog up only when invited and making sure the dog complies when asked to get down. Status can also be implied by moving the dog over on the couch before sitting down.

I like to know the answer to this question early on because sometimes during the history-taking process, a dog will jump on the couch next to me. When I ask whether it is okay for the dog to be up there, often the wife will say, "Oh, sure" as the husband answers, "Well, not really." This naturally leads to a discussion of setting consistent rules and boundaries for the dog, just as we would for kids.

*Where does the dog eliminate?*

The importance of this question is obvious when dealing with a housebreaking problem, but it can also be applicable in other situations. If a dog-aggressive dog is living in a townhome complex and eliminates in a communal, high-traffic area, suggesting an alternate elimination spot might be warranted. This question will also sometimes elicit a question from owners about whether it would be possible for the dog to eliminate in one spot in the back yard. You can then offer instructions on how to achieve that goal.

*Where is the dog kept when no one is home?*

Most owners who have dogs with housebreaking or destruction issues realize the dog must be contained when they are gone. Others, however, just haven't given it much thought. I have seen numerous clients over the years whose dogs had housebreaking issues, yet they gave those dogs free run of the house when left home alone! This is your chance to explain about baby gates, crates, and other management tools that would be appropriate.

*For what period of time, on average, is the dog left alone?*

Along with the previous question, it is important to ask how long the dog is normally left alone. While it is perfectly acceptable to leave a dog alone in a crate for three to four hours during the day, crating a dog for ten hours straight while the owner is at work is not acceptable. Ask about each family member's work or school schedule and time spent away from home so you can plan your protocol accordingly.

*What percentage of time does the dog spend indoors versus outdoors?*

Many dogs are kept outdoors when their owners are gone, and indoors when their owners are home. That is fine, so long as the outdoor area is secure and the dog has water and a shaded area. But this question could also lead to the discovery that the dog lives in the back yard full-time. Even if the owners have brought the dog inside at your request for the training session, that might be the only time the dog has ever been in the house. In that case, explain that keeping a dog outside because of housebreaking, destruction and lack of manners creates a vicious cycle, because the dog will never have the opportunity to learn those things if he is never allowed indoors!

Owners of outdoor dogs often complain about digging, barking and other behaviors that stem from boredom and a lack of physical and mental stimulation. Knowing the dog lives outdoors always prompts me to ask, "If the dog could spend time indoors without having potty accidents or causing destruction, could he be allowed in the house?" Many people respond in the affirmative. They explain that they have not had the dog indoors because the few times they tried it, the dog "ran around like a maniac." (Most never kept the dog inside long enough for that initial crazed, "Woo-hoo! I'm in the house!" period to wear off.) Or perhaps soon after bringing the dog indoors, he urinated on the carpet. These responses are your cue to explain about exercising the dog, then bringing him indoors and managing him by leashing, tethering, crating or gating off an area. Elaborate on how to proceed gradually to giving the dog more freedom in the house.

Sometimes a dog is living outdoors because the owners simply do not want dogs in the house—period. In those cases I will make a valiant attempt to explain that dogs are social, pack animals who need to be part of the family. If the owners are still adamant, I will work with them to find ways to give the dog exercise and mental stimulation, i.e., daily walks, play and attention, interactive food toys and chew bones. I know some trainers who refuse to work with dogs who live outdoors full-time. My feeling is that since the owner is calling for help rather than giving up the dog, I want to do whatever I can to make the quality of that dog and owner's relationship better. And you never know; owners have been known to change their minds as things progress, especially when they are not pressured to do so.

## Questionnaire: Training

*Has the dog had any previous training? (Describe familiar cues, training methods, and who did the training.)*

The most obvious reason to ask what cues the dog already knows is so you do not waste time and energy re-teaching them. But if an owner says the dog has had previous training, do not assume the dog knows *and will respond to* those cues. Ask specifically whether the dog will respond to learned cues reliably in the house *and* outdoors with its many distractions. Let's say Brenda tells you that Buddy knows "Come!" If you leave it at that, you might miss the fact that although Buddy understands what the word means, he will not respond to it once he has darted out the front door, when off-leash at the park, or even at times in the house with no distractions! Persevere in your questioning until you get specific information, including whether the dog will respond to the cue when given by each family member.

It is perfectly acceptable to ask owners to demonstrate skills the dog already knows. If Brenda says Buddy knows sit, down, stay and come, ask her to put him through his paces, in whatever manner she would normally use. You might find that although she says Buddy knows a certain cue, he has not practiced it since four years ago in puppy class. Also, her idea of Buddy "knowing" a cue might not be the same as yours. For example, Brenda might believe Buddy's knowing "down" means he will do it when asked, even though he pops right back up; or that Buddy lies down when asked—after being asked five times.

When responding to the "previous training" question, a client might offer the name of a trainer or training academy, or mention the methods used. That could provide a clue as to what the dog has already experienced, for better or worse. It is not necessary to ask for the specific name of a previous trainer, but it is good to know whether the client trained the dog herself, attended a group class, or had previous private training.

If an owner recites a long list of trainers who have previously tried and failed to train the dog, or makes derogatory comments about a previous trainer, consider it a red flag. Sure, there are bad trainers out there and the training failure could be on the part of the trainer or the methods used. But it is also very possible that the owner never followed through with suggestions those trainers made. Tread carefully when discussing other trainers. Do not make or agree with disparaging remarks;

doing so would only make *you* appear unprofessional. And be careful to monitor your client's progress at each session so you know she has been working with the dog. If you find vist after visit that no effort has been made, consider terminating the relationship, lest you be added to that list of failed trainers. (For more on terminating training relationships see *Miscellaneous Questions.*)

In some cases, previous training methods can explain a dog's present behavior. For example, shutting down when leashed could be a clue that the dog was previously trained with harsh leash corrections. (It could also mean the dog was seldom walked on leash or had a traumatic incident while leashed—but the shutting down is definitely a red flag that warrants further exploration.) Knowing what training methods were previously employed could also explain the owner's current training habits. For example, owners who have previously trained with leash corrections often have to be reminded to keep the leash slack as they practice. (Although the leash should have been slack in order to give a proper leash correction to begin with, many keep the leash constantly taut.) When recommending a head halter to an owner who previously trained using leash corrections, it is especially important to stress that corrections should never be used with a head halter, as they could damage the dog's neck. (For owners who cannot seem to lose the habit of jerking the leash, suggest alternate equipment.)

You might discover that an owner previously attended a group class where treat training was used, but the trainer neglected to teach owners how to wean the dogs off treats. That owner might now be opposed to the use of treats in training because she feels it produces a dog who will not respond to cues without them. If you use treats as rewards, it is now your job to explain that the last trainer was on the right track, but unfortunately did not follow through. Of course, you will explain the proper way to do so. Whatever training methods you use, be aware of what came before and instruct accordingly. Defining your starting point in this way will allow you to design a more effective training program.

*What tricks does the dog know?*

I am often impressed with the tricks novice owners have taught their dogs. Some have taught "shake" or "roll over," while others have taught the dog to "play dead," fetch objects or bark on cue. Knowing what tricks the dog already knows can come in handy when formulating solutions to behavior issues. A dog who already knows "go to bed" or "get your ball," for example, could be taught to do one of those things when the doorbell rings, rather than jumping on guests.

*Describe how you reprimand, correct, or punish your dog for unwanted behavior, and give an example of a circumstance under which you might do so.*

"Reprimand," "correction," and "punishment" are words that are subject to interpretation. One owner's reprimand might involve frowning at the dog and saying, "Eh-eh!" while another gives the dog a time out. A third might yell and slap the dog lightly on the rear, while a fourth smacks or even kicks the dog. Knowing what type of reprimands are being given and for which behaviors can afford a great opportunity to educate. It can also give valuable clues as to the dog-owner relationship, and might even provide a major key to the dog's behavior issues.

*Describe how you reward your dog for good behavior.*

Sometimes what a human considers to be rewarding is not such hot stuff to dogs! For example, an owner might pat her dog's head repeatedly or hug him as a reward, but many dogs do not appreciate these gestures. If her dog dislikes the patting, and she pats him on the head as a reward for coming to her, she will soon have a dog who does not respond when called—or stops just out of arm's reach. Ask what reward is being used and have the client demonstrate. Watch the dog's reaction carefully and offer feedback.

*Who will be responsible for training the dog?*

I cannot tell you how many times I have asked this question, only to be met with silence as kids stare blankly at parents and spouses exchange glances, each waiting for the other to volunteer. Do not assume that families have considered who will actually work with the dog. And despite your explanation on the phone that an effort will be required on their part, some people still assume the trainer is the one who will be making all the effort. Together with the family, reach a consensus on not only who will work with the dog, but when, and on which specific exercises. If you leave things up in the air, you are bound to return for the next appointment only to be met with shrugs and blank stares when you ask how training is progressing.

## Questionnaire: General Information

*What would you most like to change about your dog's behavior? Name at least three things, in order of importance.*

This is a great question, for a few reasons. First, it forces clients to clarify in their own minds what they would like to accomplish, rather than just relaying that they are frustrated with their dogs' behavior. That clarification will allow you and the client to set clear goals. Second, responses to this question often reveal that what is of great import to one family member might not be of concern to another. For example, Bonnie tells you she would most like to have Pug, the oh-so-creatively-named Pug, stop jumping on family members. Husband Rick interrupts to say he doesn't mind if Pug jumps on him; after all, the dog is just a foot tall! Son Keith volunteers that he does not like it when Pug nips. Young Katrina would simply like to take Pug for a walk without being dragged down the street. Although everyone agrees that Pug's behavior is frustrating, apparently there is not a consensus as to which behavior is the most important to modify. With your assistance, after some negotiation, an agreement is reached as to which behaviors will be addressed and in what order. Now everyone is more likely to be satisfied, and therefore compliant, as training proceeds.

*Is the dog housebroken? Crate trained?*

When working with a puppy, asking this question is a given. But it is also important whenever a client has brought an adult dog into the home. The owner might not have considered that, in a previous home, the dog might not have been allowed into the house. The other part of the question, knowing whether a dog is crate trained, is also helpful in a housebreaking discussion. If the dog is not crate trained, or the client is unfamiliar with the concept, this is an opportunity to explain why crating is such an effective management solution for housebreaking, destruction and other issues.

*What type of exercise does the dog receive?*

Be sure to get a very specific answer to this question. Often owners will offer a vague response such as, "Oh, he runs around a lot out there," while gesturing toward the back yard. Ask whether the dog gets taken for walks and if so, how often and for how long (or for what distance). A dog living in an apartment might get three walks per day, but there is a huge difference between three 30-minute walks per day and three "potty walks" that last only five to ten minutes apiece.

Ask whether the family plays games with the dog that involve fetching or chasing. Does the dog have opportunities to play with other dogs? Go to parks where he can run off-leash? Do the owners take the dog hiking or do other activities with him? Are they involved in dog sports such as agility or flyball? You will find many high-energy dogs living with owners who will not or cannot find the time, or are physically unable to provide adequate exercise. This is your chance to be creative, both in helping families to find time in their busy schedules, and by suggesting various ways to exercise the dog.

Sending the dog to doggie daycare or employing a dog-walker can be an enormous help. But even if a family cannot afford those options, there are creative solutions right at home. If the house is a two-story, the dog could chase the ball up and down the stairs. If a family member rides a bicycle, attaching the dog with a device such as a K9 Cruiser (see *Resources*) could be an option. (Always take the dog's physical condition into account when making exercise-related suggestions.)

I worked with an elderly woman once whose young Rat Terrier needed more exercise. The woman had physical limitations; long walks were out of the question. My solution included hiring a dog-walker, but I also introduced her to the Chase N' Pull Tug Toy ™ (see *Resources*). This simple yet ingenious toy looks similar to a cat toy, or a fishing pole. It consists of a long plastic rod with a sturdy rope attached, ending in a sheepskin-covered squeaky toy. I still remember the way my client's face lit up as she sat there, swishing the toy from side to side on the ground and making it jump in the air, her Rat Terrier joyfully bounding back and forth after it. If there are toys you recommend, bring a sample along and show your clients how to use the toy with their dog. Paint a picture for clients of how improved their dog's behavior will be by getting more exercise, and find ways to make it happen.

*Can you describe a typical day in the life of your dog?*

This question can be useful in gauging the amount of mental stimulation, physical exercise and socialization a dog receives on a regular basis. It can also paint a picture of the family dynamic. You might discover which family members spend the most time with the dog, how much time the dog spends contained versus free-roaming, what activities (if any) the family engages in with the dog, and whether the dog or the humans have more influence in day-to-day interactions.

*What is the dog's favorite treat? Can you name two others he enjoys?*

For a reward to be effective, it has to be something the dog likes. The more information you have about what a dog finds valuable, the more effective your training will be. Armed with that information, you might choose to use the dog's second or third favorite treat when doing training exercises in the house, and save the most valued treat to be paired with training outdoors or working around major distractions.

*What is the dog's favorite toy or game? Are there two others he enjoys?*

I know trainers who use only food treats as rewards. But in doing so, they miss out on another valuable reinforcer—the dog's favorite toy or game. When teaching a dog to come when called, a toss of the ball or a quick game of tug can be just as rewarding (and even more so for some dogs) as a food treat. A game of tug can also serve as a reward for a dog who is so aroused by the outdoor environment that he ignores food. The more types of rewards at your disposal, the more creative and effective your training can be.

*What is the dog's favorite activity?*

The dog's favorite activity might have already been mentioned in answer to the previous question, but do not assume that is the case. You might find that Barney the Beagle's favorite activity is sniffing the grass on walks. If so, you now have a valuable training reward; if Barney wants to sniff the grass, he must walk nicely by his owner's side to reach it. Perhaps chasing things is Annie the Aussie's favorite pastime. Sometimes when Annie comes when called, her reward could be chasing her owner. Again, do not limit your effectiveness by limiting types of rewards.

*What is your dog's least favorite thing?*

If an owner tells you the dog's least favorite thing is having a leash put on or riding in the car, offer tips on how to make those experiences less stressful through desensitization. If the owner of a small dog says the dog's least favorite thing is being picked up, teach the owner how to desensitize the dog to handling.

If an owner says the dog's least favorite thing is being ignored or being apart from the family, placing the dog in an isolated time-out area would likely be an effective punishment.

*Can family members handle the dog physically? Bathe him? Trim nails?*

I am sometimes surprised to find that at a session where the complaint does not involve aggression, the reply to this question is that no one can physically manipulate the dog without being growled at or even bitten. This information definitely falls into the category of Things That Are Good to Know, and alerts you that at some point the handling issue needs to be addressed. If the issue is severe, this information might even prompt you to refer the case to a behavior specialist.

*Do you plan to do any type of competition, dog sports, or therapy-related activities with your dog?*

Knowing an owner's goals will help you to streamline training. For example, the owner tells you she plans to compete in the conformation ring. In normal pet dog training, you would have the dog sit when the owner stops walking. But you might do things differently with this dog, since the automatic sit would not be desirable behavior for a dog in the show ring. You might also put more emphasis on skills the dog will need, e.g., tolerance to handling, and stand-stays. If you have clients who are interested in pursuing a dog sport or competing in the show ring, do what you can to assist—but refer them to a professional in that field as well.

# Questionnaire: Behavior Issues

Behavior issues are so varied that it would be impossible to present one comprehensive questionnaire. But whether the issue is mild or severe, the following questions will provide a good starting point. The answers you receive should, of course, be interpreted in conjunction with responses from other questionnaires.

*Can you describe the behavior?*

Be sure to get a specific description of what the dog *does*, rather than accepting the owner's assessment of the dog's motives or internal state. "The dog freaks out when we're gone" is not especially helpful. Knowing that the dog shreds a specific family member's laundry or claws grooves in the front door when left alone is solid information. You may have to calmly and repeatedly steer owners away from emotional observations to extract concrete, useful information.

---

### Exercise: Observation

Purpose: to understand how difficult it can be
to stick to facts when describing canine behavior.

This exercise involves observing dogs' body language as they interact with each other. You will need either a store-bought or home-made videotape that shows dogs interacting, or access to Animal Planet™ or a dog-related television program. Watching live interaction is fine as a last resort, but it is best if you can replay the action. As you watch the dogs interact, write down everything you see them *doing*. "The dog turned away from the other dogs, tucked his tail and ran into a crate in the corner" would be an objective observation. Saying the dog was "afraid of" or "uncomfortable with" the others would be assigning emotion. When I participated in this exercise at a seminar for trainers, I was surprised that so many trainers gave subjective, rather than objective, reports on the dogs' behavior. Practicing this exercise will improve your observational skills, help you to get clients to stick to the facts, and increase your empathy when a client has difficulty being objective!

*What would you like the dog to do instead?*

Instead of jumping on visitors, a dog could sit to be greeted; instead of begging for food at the dinner table, he could lie quietly on his bed. It is necessary for you and the owner to reach agreement as to what the dog *should* do, so that training can be properly focused. Considering this question is also a useful exercise for the owner, as it encourages the habit of seeking out proactive solutions rather than simply complaining about problems.

*When did the behavior first manifest?*

There is a big difference between a three-year-old dog whose housebreaking issue has been present since puppyhood, and one whose problem surfaced recently. The former could indicate that the owner has never bothered to address the problem until now (you can bet there's new carpeting involved), while the latter could indicate a medical or stress-related issue. There are many situations in which the answer to this question can lead to information that is crucial to solving the dog's problems.

Knowing how long a dog has been displaying a behavior can also give you an idea of how difficult that behavior might be to modify. A seven-year-old dog who has lunged and barked at other dogs on walks since puppyhood is sure to present more of a challenge than an eight-month-old pup who is just beginning to show those behaviors.

*Were there any changes in the household at the time the behavior first manifested?*

Sometimes the presentation of a dog's behavior issues coincides with the addition or loss of another pet or family member. Sometimes a change in the owner's daily schedule affects the amount of attention or exercise the dog gets, which in turn contributes to behavior issues. A behavior change might even be related to something one would not normally consider, such as the dog being stressed due to work being done on the house, loud construction work in the neighborhood, or new neighbors moving in next-door. Ask the owner whether she can recall any circumstances that might be related.

*How often does the behavior occur?*

It is important to get solid data about how often a problem behavior occurs, rather than accepting the subjective description of the owner. "It's gotten pretty bad" does not give as much information as, "He darts out the door one out of every two times it is opened for a visitor." Terms such as "pretty bad" are, of course, subjective. While one owner of a ten-week-old pup might consider the pup's daily accidents on the living room carpet to be understandable, another might find such frequent housebreaking accidents unacceptable to the point that the pup is in danger of losing his home. In accepting the subjective evaluation of these two owners, without asking how often the behavior occurred, you might get an erroneous idea of the severity of the problem. The answer to this question can open the door to a discussion of normal versus abnormal canine behavior, and what should and should not be acceptable.

Consider the importance of knowing how often a behavior occurs in a situation where budding aggression is involved. One owner might consider the adolescent dog's snapping at the children on a regular basis to be a puppy-like nuisance rather than a serious issue, while another will call for help immediately after the first incident. If you do not respond to a comment such as, "The dog snaps at the kids" by asking how often the behavior occurs, you might not make an accurate assessment of the severity of the problem.

*Under what specific circumstances does the behavior occur?*
*In what location does the behavior occur?*
*Who is present when the behavior occurs?*

This trio of questions can help to hone in on critical details. Knowing that a dog is "possessive" is not specific enough. Does the dog guard specific items? Does he guard only in a specific location, such as on the bed? Does he guard from a specific person, or from people in general? Does the behavior occur in the mornings or evenings?

"The dog is aggressive toward people." Again, this statement is not specific enough. Does the dog growl at people only on walks, or in the home as well? What does he physically *do* besides growl? Is he reactive only when being walked by a specific person? These are just a few of the many questions that should be asked. (See *Aggression Issues* for a full questionnaire.) Regardless of the problem, the more detailed, specific information you get, the greater your chance of resolving the issue.

*Has the frequency of the behavior increased, decreased, or remained the same?*
*Has the intensity of the behavior strengthened, weakened, or remained the same?*

A dog who has growled at the kids twice in his entire life, is now growling at them twice daily—that change in frequency is crucial information. If a home-alone dog used to shred laundry items now and then but is now detroying everything in his path, that change in intensity is significant. These increases in intensity and frequency alert trainers to look for contributing factors. And although you might think the answer "it's lessened" is unlikely, sometimes an owner has already attempted a solution that is beginning to help.

*When was the most recent incident?*

The answer to this question, in conjunction with the two previous questions, will form a clearer picture of what you are dealing with and the acuity of the problem. Get as much detail as possible about the most recent incident, along with detailed descriptions of previous incidents.

*What prompted you to seek help at this time?*

Depending on the nature of the issue, the answer to this question could be anything from, "Because he bit our child" to, "We're getting a new couch and we don't want him destroying it." You might be surprised at the information this question uncovers; it is always worth asking.

*What has been done so far to address the problem?*

The answer to this question can contain extremely valuable information. If the dog has an aggression issue, and punishment-based methods have been employed to "fix" the problem, it is very possible that the problem has worsened. And although the owners have called you for help, they may still be using the punishment-based methods, for lack of better options. This is your chance to educate and offer better solutions. If the owners have been on the right track and simply need a bit of direction, that is your opportunity to positively reinforce them for what they have been doing, and to help modify their approach.

You will hear all manner of replies to this question, ranging from perfectly reasonable solutions that simply did not work with a particular dog, to truly horrendous tactics that make you want to shout, "What idiot told you to do *that*?!" Whatever the answer, remain neutral and do not lay blame, lest you offend and thereby lose your opportunity to improve the situation for both dog and owner.

*How much time and effort are you willing to spend on resolving this issue?*
*Have you considered the options, should the issue not be solvable?*

These questions come into play most often with serious behavior cases. While I would not expect the owner of a Beagle who is getting into the laundry hamper to answer, "If that darn dog steals one more bra, he's out of here!" it would be reasonable for the owner of a dog who is biting visitors to seriously consider her options.

It is important for you to know your client's commitment level before proceeding with any behavior modification program. You might find that while one family member is dedicated to keeping the dog at any cost, another has reached the end of the proverbial rope; if you don't "fix" the problem quickly, the dog will lose his home and possibly his life. In cases where families are divided, you might find that one person follows your instructions, while another sits back and waits for the dog to make that final mistake. This scenario is doomed from the start. You must get an acceptable level of commitment from *all* family members before embarking on any behavior modification program. Stress the importance of that commitment in making the program successful. Ensure that each person understands how much time and effort will be involved, and how long it might take to begin seeing results.

If agreement and commitment to the program is not possible, discuss options. Some owners have not let themselves consider what would happen, should the dog's problems not be solvable. That is understandable, as those choices can be extremely difficult. Depending on the dog's issues, options might include management, rehoming (or rescue) or euthanasia. Give owners a realistic overview of each option. (For a discussion of euthanasia, see *Miscellaneous Questions*.)

## 14

# *Aggression Issues*

*To See or Not to See?*

If you are just beginning in-home training, you might not want to take on aggression cases. As previously stated, aggression issues should never be addressed unless a trainer is qualified and confident. Aggression work not only carries the risk of injury and liability, but your evaluation and prognosis could mean life or death for a dog. Many trainers refer aggression cases, preferring to focus exclusively on obedience and milder behavior issues. Never feel pressured to take on aggression work just because other trainers are doing so or because someone thinks you should. You can have a long and successful career without ever seeing a single aggression case, if you so choose.

*Laying the Foundation*

If you *are* interested in doing aggression work, you will need a solid foundation of knowledge and hands-on experience. This can be acquired through a combination of reading books, watching videos, attending seminars, volunteering with shelters or rescue groups, and best of all, apprenticing with an experienced trainer. If you apprentice with another trainer, your mentor will probably accompany you on initial in-home visits. That way she can provide backup in case you are unsure about how to proceed, step in if needed, and provide feedback.

Book knowledge alone won't cut it. If you do not have access to a mentor or the opportunity to watch other trainers work, volunteer with your local shelter or rescue organization. The hands-on experience you will gain by working with a wide range of breeds and temperaments is invaluable.

*Stay Safe*

Two pieces of advice regarding aggression work: never take a case you do not feel qualified for or that makes you uncomfortable in any way; and *stay safe*. Staying safe means controlling the environment so there is the least chance of your being injured. If the dog is contained in the back yard or another room when you arrive, or tethered to a heavy piece of furniture (with collar checked by owner so it cannot slip off over his head), you are not likely to be bitten walking in the door. Some trainers prefer that when they enter the house, the owner have the dog on a leash. Personally, I do not want a nervous owner at the end of the leash, potentially transferring that tension to the dog. Besides, most pet owners are not expert canine handlers and should the dog lunge, I would rather have a solid piece of furniture holding him back than a freaked-out human.

If at any point during a session you feel the dog's behavior is more than you can or want to handle, be honest with your client. What might have seemed a minor problem on the phone could turn out to be a major aggression issue of which the owner was not aware. *Do not ever feel you have to follow through with a session just because you are already in the person's home.* You can always tell the owner that since you have observed the dog's behavior first-hand, you feel more comfortable referring the case to another trainer. The fastest way to get hurt is to listen to your pride instead of your instincts.

Stay safe legally as well. Regardless of what type of aggression is involved, have your client sign a liability contract. (See *Appendix A.*) While it is true that the document is not guaranteed to hold up in court, the act of having signed it is often enough to dissuade a person from suing.

*Questions and Interviewing Technique*

Over the years, I have developed a mental list of questions to ask when dealing with specific types of aggression. There are so many variables when working with any behavior issue, and so many types of aggression, that it would be impossible to offer a comprehensive list of questions— but the questionnaires that appear in this chapter offer a solid starting point. The responses you get to these initial questions will determine the direction your line of questioning will take. Again, *this is not meant as encouragement to begin doing aggression work before you are truly ready.*

You will notice that many of the questions include sample answers. For example, a question in the *Aggression toward Unfamiliar People* section reads, "When you notice a person on the street, before your dog reacts, what is *your* reaction (e.g., do you become stressed, tighten up on the leash, talk to your dog)?" Do not verbalize the parts of the question that are in parenthesis. Instead, simply ask what the owner's reaction is when a person appears on the street. If the answer is general, such as "I don't really do anything" or "I get a little nervous," move to specifics such as "Do you tighten or loosen the leash?" or "Do you say anything to your dog and, if so, what does that sound like?" By following this interviewing technique, you will get accurate, specific information and will avoid putting words in your client's mouth.

*Interpreting the Answers*

You may receive answers that indicate low-level aggression in specific circumstances. Keep in mind that if a few of those circumstances were combined, the risk of biting would exponentially increase. Take a dog who guards pig ears in the kitchen but will not bite; growls when asked to get off the bed but will not bite; and dislikes being touched around the hindquarters but will not bite. If that same dog were lying on the bed with a pig ear and was lightly slapped on the hindquarters while being asked to get down, that dog might very well bite. As you can see from this example, answers must be interpreted individually *and* in conjunction with other answers to form a true picture of a dog's behavior. In addition to these questions, you will of course ask about the dog's lifestyle, i.e., nutrition, exercise, training, and other general questions.

*Topics for Discussion*

Regardless of the type of aggression you are hired to address, there are certain topics that should be discussed with your client:

*1. Origins of behavior* If appropriate, explain why the aggression might have developed. For example, Tizzy, who has been in the Livingston home since the age of seven weeks, is dog-aggressive. While taking a history, you discover that Tizzy was never socialized as a pup. It would be appropriate, without laying blame, to explain that early socialization is crucial and that the lack of it probably contributed to Tizzy's behavior. While nothing can be done to change Tizzy's early experiences at this point, the information will help the Livingstons do better in the future.

*2. Treatment plan*  Outline your strategy for dealing with the problem, explain it step by step, and explain terms and techniques clearly. Ask whether there are questions, and whether the plan seems feasible.

*3. Management*  A discussion of management should include how to keep the dog safely contained during specific times, e.g., around visitors, or when the children are running and playing. If proper management is not in place, progress cannot be made and the risk of liability is high.

4. *Ground rules*  Ensure that clients understand the rules for everyday interactions with their dog. Ground rules might include clearing and keeping the living space free of specific triggers (e.g., pig ears). These rules should be tailored to the client's particular situation. For example, "If Duke steals Billy's toy, Billy should call Mom instead of trying to take the toy back." Explain to *all* owners the importance of the rule, "If the dog growls, he should not be confronted or punished." Growling is a symptom, not a problem; it is a dog's way of saying he is uncomfortable with something. Should that option be eliminated, the dog might bite with no warning. Explain that walking away as though disgusted and ignoring the dog does not mean the dog is in charge, but is a way of avoiding confrontation while the problem is being addressed.

5. *Emergency tactics*  Teach clients what to do in an emergency. For example, "If Buddy grabs something he absolutely should not have (e.g., a chicken bone stolen from the trash), run to the fridge and grab a handful of treats. Make a big deal of scattering them on the floor. When Buddy drops the chicken bone to go after the treats, quietly pick up the bone." Again, although you are working on addressing the actual issue, confrontation must be avoided in the meantime.

6. *Aggression is not "easily curable."*  Stress this to all clients who are dealing with aggression issues. It would be misleading to let an owner believe that her dog's issues will be resolved in one or two sessions. Sure, she might have all the information needed to continue working with the dog by then, but it could take weeks to see any progress, and months to really resolve the issue. It should be stressed that although a dog's behavior can be greatly modified, aggression is never "cured" and is something owners must be vigilant about throughout the dog's life.

## Questionnaires - Aggression

The following questionnaires are broken down into specifc types of aggression. Not all types of aggression are covered. See *Appendix C* for books on dealing with various types of aggression.

### Handling Issues

(If the dog is reactive toward handling by the owners, check for other owner-directed aggression including resource guarding.)

1. Does the dog have any medical problems? Is he on medication? If so, what medication, at what dosage and for how long?

2. How long have you had the dog and how long has this been an issue?

3. Has the dog been neutered? If so, when?

4. On vet visits, can staff physically handle dog? Must he be muzzled?

5. At the groomcr, can staff physically handle dog? Must he be muzzled'?

6. Has the dog ever bitten or tried to bite the vet, vet staff or groomer?

7. Is the dog sensitive to fast or overhead movements?

8. Will the dog accept petting and handling from all family members, when they initiate the interaction (as opposed to his soliciting the attention)?

9. For each of the following, will the dog allow all family members to perform the activity? What about strangers? What percentage of the time? What is the dog's reaction?

   a. Reach for dog
   b. Pat top of head
   c. Lean over dog
   d. Step over dog
   e. Pick up dog
   f. Push dog (e.g., shoving over on couch)

g.  Bathe dog
h.  Brush dog
i.  Pull fur (including tail)
j.  Check teeth
k.  Check/clean ears
l.  Clip nails
m.  Grab collar
n.  Pull by collar (e.g., to move off couch)
o.  Attach leash to collar
p.  Hug
q.  Restrain (is reaction specific to body part such as paws or head?)

10. Is the dog less accepting of touch on a specific body part?

11. Is the dog less accepting of touch when he is in a specific position (e.g., lying down)?

12. Is the dog less accepting of touch when he is in a specific location (e.g., on couch or bed)?

13. Is the dog less accepting of touch at a specific time (e.g., evenings, or upon being awakened)?

14. Is the dog less accepting of touch when he is in possession of food or another highly valued item?

15. Would you say this behavior has become more frequent and/or intense, or stayed the same? If more frequent/intense, since when? Was there a specific incident or circumstance that preceded or coincided with this increase?

16. Has the dog ever been punished for growling or giving other warning signals?

17. Has the dog ever bitten or tried to bite anyone? If so, describe each incident in detail.

18. What has been done to address this issue so far? Describe results.

19. Can you offer any other information that might be helpful?

## Resource Guarding

(If the dog has resource guarding issues check for handling issues—many dogs with resource guarding issues have handling issues as well.)

1. Does the dog have any medical problems? Is he on medication? If so, what medication, at what dosage and for how long?

2. How long have you had the dog and how long has this been an issue?

3. Has the dog been neutered? If so, when?

4. What item(s) does the dog guard (e.g., dry or wet food, toys, balls, treats, chew bones, "forbidden" items such as tissues or socks)?

5. Does the dog guard his food, food bowl, water dish or feeding area?

6. Is this behavior more intense in a specific location (e.g., on bed, in back yard, under a table)? (Despite the fact that this is a serious issue, I can't help hearing Dr. Seuss reciting, *"I will not bite him on a train, I will not bite him on a plane…"*)

7. Does the dog guard items that are not actually in his possession (e.g., food on countertop, food that has been dropped on floor, bone that has been buried in couch cushions)?

8. Does the dog guard a specific person or people (become reactive when others approach the person/people)?

9. Does the dog guard a specific location (i.e., he guards the location itself—such as owner's bed or a doorway)?

10. When the dog has a valued item, what is his reaction if someone approaches? Describe physical reaction as specifically as possible (e.g., stiffening of body, freezing, hard eye, growling, air-snapping).

11. How closely can a person approach before eliciting this response? Can the person stroke the dog? Reach toward the item?

12. What do family members do when the dog shows this reaction (e.g.,

retreat, take the item, reprimand, or "punish" the dog)? What is the dog's reaction?

13. Has the dog ever been punished for growling or giving other warning signals?

14. Who does the dog guard from? Is his reaction stronger with a certain family member?

15. Does the dog guard items from strangers?

16. Does the dog guard more intensely or more frequently from one specific type of person (i.e., man, woman, child)?

17. Would you say this behavior has become more frequent and/or intense, or stayed the same? If more frequent/intense, since when? Was there a specific incident or circumstance that preceded or coincided with this increase?

18. Has the dog ever bitten a person who attempted to take an item from him? If so, describe each incident including approximate date, specific circumstances, who was present, number of bites, severity of bite(s), and what occurred right before and right after the bite(s).

19. Is there a time of day or other specific circumstance under which the dog is more likely to guard this item (e.g., only in the evenings, if he has not been exercised that day, if another dog is present)?

20. What has been done to address this issue so far? Describe results.

21. Can you offer any other information that might be helpful?

## Aggression toward Unfamiliar People

There are many environments and circumstances in which a dog might become aggressive toward strangers, such as in the car or at a crowded outdoor event. The following questions focus on two of the most common scenarios: aggression toward people while on a walk, and aggression when an unfamiliar person enters the home (with owners present).

## Aggression toward Unfamiliar People on Walks

1. Does the dog have any medical problems? Is he on medication? If so, what medication, at what dosage and for how long?

2. Has the dog been neutered? If so, when?

3. How long have you had the dog and how long has this been an issue?

4. Is the dog sensitive to sound, touch or movement?

5. With what type of collar and leash is the dog being walked?

6. Is the dog always leashed for walks or is he allowed off-leash?

7. What is the dog's reaction to strangers on a walk? Describe physical reaction as specifically as possible (e.g., freezes, backs up, barks, growls, snarls, lunges forward, piloerection, air-snapping).

8. What percentage of the time does this reaction occur?

9. Does this reaction differ depending on who is present or who is holding the leash?

10. Is the dog's reaction stronger with one type of person, (e.g., adult male, female, child—if so, give age range—elderly? Skin color? Facial hair?)

11. At what distance does this reaction take place?

12. Is this reaction dependent on the stranger's angle of approach (e.g.,

walking horizontally across the field of vision vs. coming toward the dog)?

13. Is this reaction different if the stranger is walking a dog? If so, how?

14. Are there specific items or motions that trigger this reaction (e.g., hat, sunglasses, cane, walking with limp, waving arms)?

15. Does the dog react to people running, bicycling, skateboarding, or other movement-oriented activities?

16. Is the reactivity to people stronger in a specific location (e.g., the dog's own neighborhood)? Is the reaction present outside the dog's own territory and to what degree?

17. Does the dog's reaction to strangers differ depending on the time of day? If so, how?

18. If there is another dog in the home, is this dog's behavior different when the other dog is present? If so, how?

19. When you notice a person on the street, before your dog reacts, what is *your* reaction (e.g., become stressed, tighten up on the leash, talk to your dog)?

20. Do you currently ask your dog to do anything when he sees a person on the street (e.g., move to the side, look at you, sit)?

21. What do you normally do once your dog has reacted to a stranger (e.g., pull him closer, reprimand or "correct" him, make him sit, redirect his attention, walk away)?

22. Would you say this behavior has become more frequent and/or intense, or stayed the same? If more frequent/intense, since when? Was there a specific incident or circumstance that preceded or coincided with this increase?

23. Can people ever approach and/or pet your dog on walks? Specify what type of people (i.e., adults, children, women) and under what circumstances (e.g., okay if dog approaches them).

24. Has your dog ever bitten a person? If so, how many incidents have there been? Describe each incident, including approximate date, specific circumstances, who was present, number of bites, severity of bite(s), and what occurred right before and right after the bite(s).

25. What has been done to address this issue so far? Describe results.

26. Can you offer any other information that might be helpful?

## Aggression toward Unfamiliar People in the Home

1. Does the dog have any medical problems? Is he on medication? If so, what medication, at what dosage and for how long?

2. Has the dog been neutered? If so, when?

3. How long have you had the dog and how long has this been an issue?

4. Is the dog sensitive to sound, touch, or movement?

5. Where is the dog normally kept when a new person comes to the door (e.g., behind a gate, back yard, loose in the house)?

6. Does the dog have visual access to people passing the house (e.g., standing on chair looking out window)? Does he react? If so, describe.

7. What is the dog's reaction to the doorbell, and to knocking?

8. What does the dog do when an unfamiliar person arrives? Describe physical reaction in detail. (This question should have been answered in detail on the phone as well. Never accept a vague "he's fine" when you are to be the next person in the door.) Get specifics (e.g., freezing, lunging, piloerection, staring, growling, barking, snarling, air-snapping, biting). What do you do if your dog has this reaction?

9. If the dog is kept in the yard, what does he do when an unfamiliar person enters the yard? Describe physical reaction in specific detail.

10. With what percentage of visitors does the dog have this reaction?

11. Are there any specific items or motions that trigger this reaction (e.g., hat, sunglasses, cane, gesturing)?

12. Is the dog's reaction stronger with one type of person (e.g., male, female, child—give age range—elderly? Skin color? Facial hair?)?

13. Is the dog's reaction to strangers different depending on time of day? If so, how?

14. Is dog's reaction the same regardless of who (family) is present?

15. When reacting, does the dog move toward or away from the visitor?

16. Does dog's reaction to a visitor lessen with repeated exposures?

17. Has the dog ever bitten a visitor? If so, how many incidents have there been? Describe each, including approximate date, specific circumstances, who was present, number of bites, location and severity of bite(s), and what occurred right before and right after the bite(s).

18. Once visitors are in the home, does the dog warm up to them and if so, how long does it normally take?

19. Can visitors eventually pet your dog? Is there any specific type of petting that elicits a reaction?

20. If a visitor stands up, re-enters a room, or walks away, does the dog react? If so, how?

21. Does the dog react if a visitor approaches or interacts with (e.g., hugs) a specific family member?

22. Does the dog react if visitor approaches a certain location or resource?

23. If there is another dog in the home, is this dog's behavior different when the other dog is present? If so, how?

24. If the dog growls or otherwise warns visitors once in the home, what is your reaction, and how does the dog respond to your actions?

25. Is the dog managed in any way when visitors are present?

26. Would you say this behavior has become more frequent and/or intense, or stayed the same? If more frequent/intense, how long? Did a specific incident or circumstance precede or coincide with this increase?

27. What has been done to address the issue so far? Describe results.

28. Can you offer any other information that might be helpful?

## Aggression toward Unfamiliar Dogs

1. Does the dog have any medical problems? Is he on medication? If so, what medication, at what dosage and for how long?

2. Has the dog been neutered? If so, when?

3. How long have you had the dog and how long has this been an issue?

4. Is the dog sensitive to sound, touch, or movement?

5. With what type of collar and leash is the dog being walked?

6. Is the dog always leashed for walks or is he allowed off-leash?

7. How often is the dog taken for walks and for what length of time?

8. Was the dog exposed to other dogs as a pup? How did he interact with them?

9. If there are other dogs in the home, do the dogs fight with each other?

10. Are there any dogs your dog currently plays with or with whom he is comfortable (other than your own dogs)?

11. At home, does the dog have access to see other dogs going past the house (e.g., by standing on the couch looking out the window, looking through back yard gate)? If so, what is his reaction when a dog passes?

12. Has the dog ever been attacked by another dog?

13. When he is taken for a walk, what is the dog's reaction to other dogs? Describe physical reaction as specifically as possible.

14. In what percentage of exposures to other dogs does this reaction occur?

15. At what distance from other dogs does this reaction occur?

16. Is the dog's reaction more intense when encountering a specific characteristic in another dog (e.g., male, female, neutered,

unneutered, large, small, prick-eared, stub tail, tail curved over back, specific color, or breed)?

17. Are there any specific actions that trigger this reaction (e.g., unfamiliar dog barking, whining, staring, wagging tail, moving toward your dog)?

18. Does this reaction occur whether the unfamiliar dog is on the street or behind a fence?

19. Is this reaction displayed only on walks in a specific area (e.g., dog's own neighborhood)? Is it present outside the dog's own neighborhood and if so, to what degree?

20. When *you* see another dog on the street, what is *your* reaction (e.g., become stressed, tighten up on the leash, talk to your dog)?

21. Does the dog's reaction differ depending on which family members are present and/or who is at the end of the leash?

22. If there is another dog in the home, is this dog's behavior different when the other dog is present? If so, how?

23. Does this reaction differ depending on the unfamiliar dog's angle or speed of approach (e.g., walking horizontally across the field of vision vs. moving directly toward your dog, walking vs. running)?

24. Would you say this behavior has become more frequent and/or intense, or stayed the same? If more frequent/intense, since when? Was there a specific incident or circumstance that preceded or coincided with this increase?

25. Do you currently ask your dog to do anything when he sees a person on the street (e.g., move to the side, look at you, sit, walk away)?

26. Is your dog ever allowed to approach and greet other dogs on walks? If so, describe which dog normally approaches, your dog's reaction, whether you tighten or loosen the leash for introductions, which types of dogs this is successful with, and who is walking your dog when successful approaches occur.

27. Does your dog "warm up" to other dogs with repeated exposures?

28. Do you let your dog off-leash at the park or elsewhere? If so, describe his interactions with other dogs when off-leash.

29. Has your dog ever fought with another dog? If so, how many incidents have there been? Please describe all incidents, including approximate date and location of incident, specific circumstances, who was present, whether the dogs were separated or ended the fight themselves, and injuries to either dog.

30. What has been done to address the issue so far? Describe results.

31. Can you offer any other information that might be helpful?

*15*

# Separation Anxiety

I have received calls over the years from owners who were sure their dogs had "separation anxiety." In the majority of those cases, it turned out the dogs were simply suffering from a lack of mental and physical stimulation, which manifested as destructive behavior, barking, or other symptoms when left alone. Unfortunately, some owners (and even professionals) assume that a dog who shows these symptoms is stressed by the owner's absence. I even had one client whose veterinarian prescribed clomipramine (a drug commonly prescribed for separation anxiety) because when left alone, the dog had chewed a shoe! Not only had the vet not discussed behavior modification (even the manufacturer recommends behavior modification in conjunction with the drug), but in this case the medication was completely unnecessary.

Separation issues range from mild to true, clinical-level separation anxiety. As with aggression, the dog may be in danger of losing his home should a solution not be found. Having owners set up a video camera to record the dog's activities when they are gone can be of great assistance in your evaluation. In the case of mild separation issues, increasing the dog's exercise, providing ways to keep busy and mentally stimulated, building up gradually to longer separations, and a variety of other strategies can help.

While true separation anxiety is not as common, you may encounter some cases. While medication can be helpful for some of these dogs, it is not your place to prescribe. If warranted, suggest owners discuss the issue with their vet, so medication can be administered in conjunction with your behavior modification protocol.

You might choose to refer cases involving separation anxiety. This section is not meant to encourage you to take them on, nor is it meant as an instructional guide to treating this complex behavior issue. As with aggression, the questionnaire is offered as a starting point. See *Appendix C* for books that specifically address separation anxiety.

## Questionnaire: Separation Anxiety

For the purpose of this questionnaire, it is assumed that you already know the dog's breed, age and health status.

1.  Where did the dog come from?

2.  Is there any background information? If there was a known previous owner, why was the dog given up? How much time did that owner spend with the dog daily?

3.  How long have you had the dog? How long has this been a problem?

4.  What type of food is the dog fed? *(You are asking this because of the nutrition/behavior link.)*

5.  Where does the dog sleep? If in the bedroom, on the bed or on the floor?

6.  Are there other pets in the home? If so, give species, breed, age and gender, and whether the other pet(s) have separation issues.

7.  Who else lives in the home and what are their normal work/school schedules?

8.  How many hours per day is the dog left alone?

9.  Is this a regular schedule or does it vary?

10. Are any electronic devices turned on when you leave the home (e.g., house alarm, dishwasher, washer/dryer)?

11. When you are at home, is the dog always in the room with you?

12. Is the dog exercised before you leave? If so, describe type of exercise, duration, and whether it tires him out. What exercise does the dog get at other times?

13. Is the dog left with any chew items while you are gone? If so, specify.

14. Where is the dog left when no one is home? Is he crated, penned or otherwise confined?

15. If there is another dog or cat in the home, are they left together when you are gone?

16. Have you ever left your dog to play with another dog (e.g., at doggie daycare or a friend's house)? If so, did he show his usual separation symptoms? If so, were they more or less intense than usual, or the same? Did they last for more or less time than usual, or the same?

17. Describe your interaction with the dog before you leave the house (e.g., "I pet him for ten minutes and tell him to be good" or, "I ignore him for the last half hour").

18. Is there a specific point in your departure routine at which the dog begins to show signs of stress (e.g., when you blow-dry hair, pick up keys)? If so, what does he do? What is your reaction?

19. Does the dog urinate or scent-mark when left alone? If so, in what location or on what specific objects? Does this behavior also occur when family members are at home?

20. Does the dog chew or destroy things when left alone? If so, specify which items and if applicable, who the items belong to (e.g., wife's laundry items). Does he make a bed of these items?

21. Does the dog drool, whine, howl or bark when left alone? If so, describe, and note (whine/howl/bark) pattern/duration if possible.

22. Does the dog engage in self-mutilating behavior when left alone (e.g., chew at himself)? If so, is he crated at the time?

23. Does the dog scratch/claw at doors, windows or other specific areas when left alone? Through which door does the owner normally exit?

24. Does the dog display these behaviors every time he is left alone?

25. If the answer to the previous question is no, how long can the dog be left alone before the behaviors manifest?

26. Does the dog display these behaviors only when a particular person leaves (e.g., dog is calm when left home with wife, but stressed if left home with husband)?

27. Does anyone come home to spend time with or walk the dog during the day? If not, can you think of anyone who might be willing to do so? Would hiring someone to do so be possible as a short-term solution, while the problem is being addressed?

28. Is a radio or television left playing when the dog is left alone? If so, is it normally playing when you are at home?

29. Describe your typical routine upon returning home, including how you greet the dog, and the dog's reaction.

30. Do you have vacation time (or do the kids have time off from school) in which it would be possible to practice gradual separations?

31. What have you tried so far to address the problem? Describe in detail and describe results, if any.

32. Can you provide any other information that might be helpful?

# Part V

# *The Session*

*16*

# The Session is Now in Order!

Regardless of whether your session will involve behavior issues, obedience training, or puppy problems, it should have a loosely planned structure. For example, your initial session should include information gathering, formulating a plan, possibly working with the dog, and discussing how to follow up.

*What's the Plan, Stan?*

Once you have taken a history, summarize the main and lesser issues for your client. Congratulate her on any work done with the dog so far and be clear on what you feel is most important to focus on immediately. For example, "The issues that should be addressed immediately are Boomer's darting out the door and not coming when called. Door-darting is a life-threatening issue, since Boomer could get hit by a car. It's great that you've already taught him to sit; that will be useful as part of the solution." Then go on to address secondary issues: "Now, you've also mentioned that you'd like Boomer to lie on his bed while your family eats dinner, and we can accomplish that as well. For now, Boomer can be tethered on his bed at mealtimes; after we address the more pressing issues, we'll work on his down-staying on his bed during meals. How does that sound?" If you do not take the time to summarize in this manner before starting the actual training, your client might be left wondering why some of her concerns have not been addressed.

Be sure your client agrees not only with which issues are most important, but with your treatment plan. You might consider a fifty-step protocol to modify the dog's resource-guarding issues brilliant, but if the client doesn't follow it, you might as well use it to line the bottom of a bird cage. Melanie, for example, has three kids, a husband, two dogs and a cat. It is likely that Melanie would find a protocol that would take 30 minutes a day overwhelming. In her case, creating a simplified plan that will work with her schedule is crucial.

Stan, on the other hand, is an electrical engineer whose eyes light up like a kid at Christmas when you discuss the minute building blocks of a fifty-step protocol. Great! Review it step by step to be sure Stan understands, then let him have at it. (Of course, you will be available to coach him along.) Know your clients. If you are not sure whether something is workable, ask.

## *What's the Problem?*

Sometimes you will find that the issue *you* find most pressing is one the client does not even consider problematic. Last year, a woman named Jeannie called for help with Mitzi, her ten-month-old Cocker Spaniel. Jeannie's main complaint was that Mitzi was a food thief. Jeannie's kids often ate dinner in front of the television, and if they left the room even for a moment—presto! The food vanished from the coffee table faster than a man from a shopping mall. Jeannie also mentioned that Mitzi did not walk well on leash, dug in the back yard, and committed a few other minor infractions.

Soon after arriving at Jeannie's home, it became obvious that Mitzi had a much bigger problem than being a food thief; she was not comfortable with strangers and was well on her way to developing a fear-based aggression issue. While I did address the food-stealing in the first session, I also made it very clear to Jeannie that Mitzi's budding aggression issue was of the utmost concern. In fact, it probably played a part in why she was not walking nicely on leash. ("Oh!" Jeannie exclaimed, "She *does* lunge toward people and bark, now that you mention it!") We decided to concentrate on Mitzi's issues with people before proceeding with anything else. It was important in gaining Jeannie's compliance that while I made her aware of the most pressing issue, I did not discount or ignore the ones she felt were important.

For behavior issues, your treatment plan will probably include a combination of management and training. For example, a dog who jumps on visitors could be leashed or tethered when visitors arrive, with visitors instructed to approach only when the dog is sitting. Explain to your client that the dog must be prevented from practicing the unwanted behavior. Even if visitors do not pet the dog when he jumps—which would be rewarding—the act of jumping on people is self-rewarding and will become habitual. This temporary management solution would go hand in hand with training sessions to teach the dog an alternate behavior. For example, you could work on having the dog sit to be greeted (without being tethered), or teach the dog to go to bed, lie down and stay whenever the doorbell rings.

Again, always ask your client whether a plan sounds feasible. If the client finds a suggestion problematic, within reason, make adjustments. Although your demeanor should be professional and authoritative, it should also be friendly enough that your clients feel comfortable telling you when something does not seem workable. While some aspects of solutions are absolutely not negotiable ("No, you may *not* have your aggressive dog off-leash at the park!"), most behavior problems have a variety of solutions. It is your job to find one that is workable for both you and your clients.

*Are We There Yet?*

In addition to letting clients know what a solution will entail, be realistic about how long training will take and how much effort will be involved. For example, at the first session with Bill and Nancy, you have determined that Biff the Boxer has a few minor behavior issues and needs a bit of obedience training. You have discussed the need for more exercise and better nutrition, outlined which skills should be taught, and discussed how the behavior issues will be addressed. It is important to ensure that Bill and Nancy understand what will be involved in daily training practice and length of the overall process. You might explain that by the end of five sessions they will have had enough practice to continue the training on their own. Between those sessions, they will be expected to work with Biff daily, aiming for five five-minute training sessions per day. Biff's new skills will soon become assimilated into their daily routine, through simple practices such as asking Biff to sit before meals. Of course, you will be available to work through extra sessions if needed. Since Bill and Nancy now have a realistic idea of what level of commitment to expect financially and time-wise, Biff's training is more likely to be successful.

You might be tempted to downplay the amount of time and effort it will take clients and their dogs to master certain skills. Don't do it! It is better to be honest and explain that certain skills (leash work and a reliable recall come to mind) involve more time and effort than simpler exercises like sit and down. That way your clients will not be frustrated when the dog has not mastered a difficult exercise after a week. You can also use management (e.g., a head halter for a dog who pulls) in the meantime to alleviate the severity of the problem immediately.

Years ago, I worked with a sprightly senior citizen named Rita. Her biggest issue with Robbie, an adorable adolescent Westie, was that his pulling on leash made it difficult for her to walk him. Robbie was small but strong! Our first session went well. We discussed alternate forms of exercise for Robbie and practiced some leash skills. Robbie did well and Rita was pleased. But when I returned for our second session a week later, Rita was distressed. While Robbie's walking had improved somewhat, he still pulled! It was my fault for not having explained that getting Robbie to walk nicely on leash was not going to happen in a week. His pulling habit was already established, so it might take a few weeks or more to get him to reliably walk next to her, especially when encountering distractions. Once Rita understood this, she was relieved. She worked with Robby daily, and I am pleased to report that after three weeks, Robbie was walking nicely next to her on their daily strolls.

Be straightforward about the level of success you feel can be achieved. It is important for an owner to know whether you feel a behavior issue can be completely resolved, and if not, what level of success can realistically be expected. For example, an eight-year-old Akita who has been dog-aggressive all his life is not likely to end up romping happily off-leash with other dogs once your training is complete. It would, however, be reasonable to expect that the dog will walk down the street nicely without lunging at other dogs. I know a trainer who uses a scale to rate a dog's prognosis; it ranges from poor to excellent. However you explain your prognosis and recommended protocol, be sure your client understands your expectations for her dog's behavior.

## Checking In

Always start a session by following up on suggestions made at the previous session. Consult your notes and ask specific questions to check progress, point by point. While it might be reinforcing to have the question, "How are things going?" answered with a resounding, "Great!", that does not offer much information. You might ask instead, "Which of the solutions we discussed for nipping have you found useful?" or, "How often does Biff nip now as compared to two weeks ago?"

It can also helpful to ask, "What *didn't* work for you?" Some people are hesitant to complain, and you will not find out if something has not been effective unless you ask. It is not enough to know that a solution did not work; you must find out *why* it did not work. In the case of behavior issues, ask the client to describe as specifically as possible what she tried and how the dog reacted. It might be that your instructions were carried out to the letter but the solution was not the right one for that particular dog. In that case, offer an alternate solution. It is also possible that the client did not understand or carry out your instructions properly. For example, you had asked that each time Bootsy nips, Nora leave the room and ignore him for two to five minutes. But upon questioning, you find that when Nora left the room, Bootsy whined and barked, so she returned immediately. Unfortunately, this taught Bootsy that whining and barking brings Nora back. Once you have explained this dynamic, reiterate the original plan step by step to be sure Nora understands. If she is absolutely not willing or able to follow the instructions, an alternate solution should be found.

Sometimes a client will decide that one of your solutions does not work and will come up with an alternate solution on her own. Continuing with our nipping example, Nora tells you she got tired of trying the solution you suggested and now when Bootsy nips, she simply holds his mouth shut. Although you might be inwardly groaning, explain neutrally why Plan B is not the best solution, then review the original plan to see where things went awry. If necessary, make an alternate suggestion.

Take care that your clients do not feel they are being put on the spot or tested by this questioning process. Done properly, it can yield valuable information that can cue you to adjust your plan if necessary, thereby keeping the training process on track.

In the case of obedience exercises, ask how the exercise has been progressing. If the client responds that things are going well, ask her to demonstrate. (Be sure to ask in a pleasant, "Would you like to show me?" tone rather than demanding, "Let's see it!") This demonstration will alert you if adjustments need to be made, and allow you to give positive feedback on how well your client and her dog are doing. If she says things are not going well, review, coach and make adjustments as necessary to ensure that she can carry out the exercises successfully.

*Take Note!*

At the beginning of each session, suggest clients have paper and pen handy to take notes, even if the topics you will cover are on handouts. When I first started training, I jotted down notes for clients, then handed them over at the end of the session. Upon hearing this, a trainer friend asked why I was working so hard; after all, shouldn't the client make some effort? She was right. Besides, this way clients can not only make notes on what they find most important, but they will actually be able to decipher those notes later on!

Taking notes is especially important at the first session, since a lot of general information is discussed. Notes should also be made after each training exercise. Each time you finish an exercise, summarize key points so your client can jot them down. For example: "Nancy, we've practiced the sit not only with Biff facing you, but also with him by your side. Practice with *you* in different positions too, like sitting, lying down, and standing  but facing away from Biff. Practice in different rooms, in the back yard, and then outdoors on walks. And remember, Biff should sit before meals, walks and anything else he finds valuable." Now when her husband comes home from work, Nancy can share the finer points with him, whereas without the notes she might not remember everything.

You should also make notes as the session progresses. For example, if you have just finished mentioning types of chew bones and other things to keep the dog busy, you would make the notation "chew bones." That way you know the subject was covered. If you have recommended the client switch dog foods, take the dog for two walks daily and stop letting the dog on the bed, write it all down.

Always record not only what recommendations were made, but what exercises were covered and what you plan to cover at the next session. If you see ten to twenty clients per week, what are the chances you will remember what you taught each one? Taking notes keeps you on track: you will always know where things left off, what to work on next and which recommendations might need following up. It is also a good idea to keep track of which handouts you have given clients.

*The Wrap-Up*

In the next chapter we will discuss structuring training sequences. For now, let's fast forward. After finishing your last training exercise of the lesson, ask whether there are questions about anything that has been covered. Reiterate the most important points. This allows you to make sure everything has been understood and leaves the information fresh in your client's mind. Be sure your client understands specifically how and when to practice between sessions. For example, "Have Biff practice down-stays during television commercials, while you get dressed in the morning, and while you are preparing dinner."

*Timing is Everything*

It is crucial to keep track of the time during sessions, so you do not go into overtime and arrive late for subsequent appointments. If you find keeping track of time challenging, wear a watch with an alarm, set for ten minutes before the end of the lesson. That ten-minute buffer will allow you to wrap up the exercise on which you are working, collect payment and set the next appointment. An alternative, if you are doing single sessions, is to collect payment and schedule the following appointment at the *beginning* of each session. That way you can work right up until the last minute. If it is the first session and you will be explaining package deals, leave yourself as much time as necessary to do so and for the client to review the contract and make payment.

In some cases, especially with complex behavior issues, you might find that you need more time to complete the lesson than was initially estimated. If time is available, tell your clients that you are happy to continue if they would like, and inform them of any extra charges that will apply.

Once you have completed the lesson, set your next appointment. Unless you are working with a serious behavior issue that warrants a few weeks between sessions for behavior modification, there is no advantage in allowing too much time to elapse between sessions. You do not want the training to lose momentum, nor clients to become lax about training practice. I set appointments approximately a week apart.

As I am leaving, I tell clients that if they have any questions between sessions to call me any time. (Well, not *any* time—at four a.m. I won't have any useful answers.) I want to know if a client meets with an unexpected reaction from the dog or is having difficulty with an exercise. You might think this practice has all the makings of a nightmare, with clients calling incessantly day and night. In my experience, most people do not abuse the privilege. Offering to act as a "technical support line" between sessions shows your concern and, in the long run, will make training more effective.

Next, we'll discuss ways to structure your training sessions for maximum efficiency.

# *Obedience Lesson Guidelines*

Behavior issues are so varied that it would be impossible to offer an individual lesson plan for each one. On the other hand, there are basic rules that apply to structuring any obedience training session. The guidelines that follow are designed to keep your sessions running smoothly and efficiently.

*Order in the House!*

Before you begin a lesson, take a moment to decide which exercises you plan to cover and in what order. The sequence in which you work training exercises can help or hinder progress.

As a general rule, train active exercises at the beginning of a lesson and more sedentary ones toward the end. Let's drop in on your second training session with Shamus the Shetland Sheepdog. You have decided to work on the recall, the down-stay and "leave it." Shamus has lots of energy and is rarin' to go when you arrive, so you begin with a recall exercise. This particular exercise involves family members standing in a circle, taking turns calling Shamus. He runs enthusiastically from person to person, sitting and being rewarded with treats each time. Since you have instructed family members to move farther apart as the game progresses, Shamus has run longer and longer distances and has done some fabulous recalls. Now it is time for a break. This will allow Shamus to rest so he can be ready for the next exercise, and the family to regroup, make notes and ask questions.

While Shamus is resting, explain how to continue working on the exercise during the week. Your clients should jot this information down. Then go on to explain the next exercise—in this case, "leave it." After teaching Shamus the exercise, giving family members feedback as they practice, summarizing key points and answering questions, the exercise is complete. You now move on to the last exercise of the lesson, the down-stay. Since Shamus is pleasantly tired out from the previous activities, he is now a lot more likely to stay down as compared to the beginning of the lesson, when he was still doing his Tasmanian Devil impersonation. Shamus' family is impressed at how long he remains in the down position. Shamus is happy to rest and receive treats!

Sequence exercises carefully. Some naturally build on others, so the order will be obvious. If you teach down from a sitting position, for example, it is logical that sit must be taught before down. But be careful; sometimes the order of a sequence can account for a dog's failure to perform an exercise. In fact, there are some exercises that should *never* be done in succession, such as "touch" and "leave it." Teaching a dog to "touch"—to target your hand by touching it with his nose—can be helpful in a variety of situations. It can teach a dog to walk in a loose heel position, serve as an alternative to lunging at other dogs, and give fearful dogs more confidence when interacting with people. Let's say you have just completed seven successful repetitions of Diamond the Doberman touching his nose to your hand. Everyone thinks Diamond is brilliant— and you're looking pretty good, too.

Next, you decide to teach "leave it," which involves presenting your hand closed tightly around a piece of food, and waiting for Diamond to *back off* the offered hand. Diamond does not back off, but instead keeps pressing his nose to your hand. Has Diamond suddenly lost his luster? What could the problem be? Since you have just finished conditioning Diamond to *touch* the hand that is presented, he is unlikely to suddenly start *backing off* the offered hand. Set everyone up to succeed by sequencing exercises wisely.

The only thing more important than formulating a lesson plan is the ability to be flexible within that plan. If your client's babysitter flaked out, leaving two young kids in the room in which you are training, postponing teaching the down-stay until the next session might be wise. If a dog spent the morning at the groomer and is low on energy, perhaps recalls or other high-energy exercises would be best saved until the next session; on the other hand, this might be a good time to address the down-stay. The mental and physical state of both dog and client, and unexpected distractions, should always be taken into consideration.

*Show and Tell*

It is important, especially when working with new clients, that they see success early on. It is all too easy to get caught up in explanations and theories as your client stands there glassy-eyed, wondering when you are going to actually *do* something with the dog. (Again, this does not apply to behavior issues, but to obedience training; at initial behavior consults you will probably do more conversing and less working with the dog.) Do a fast, easy exercise first. Once the client has observed the dog learning from you and successfully performing an exercise, her confidence in you will make her much more likely to comply with your suggestions.

When training any new exercise, work with the dog first. Explain what you are doing as you go, so the client can focus on the most important points. Do not use complicated scientific jargon; keep explanations brief and simple. For example, as you lure Diamond into a down from a sit position, you might say, "Notice how I'm keeping the treat to Diamond's nose like a magnet. I'm moving it in a straight line from his nose to the ground, rather than pulling it toward me. If I did that, Diamond might stand up to follow the treat."

Never assume that just because a client has watched you perform an exercise, that she is capable of carrying it out correctly. Have you ever watched a demonstration and felt that you understood how to perform the activity, then tried it, only to discover that while your eyes were watching, your brain had apparently snuck out for margaritas? That's how your clients sometimes feel. Although people learn in different ways, some preferring to hear new material and some to view it, most people do best when going through the motions. Regardless of how well clients say they understand an exercise, coach them through it, giving instructions as they proceed through each step.

*Troubleshooting*

Diamond performed well when you lured him into a down. But when you turn him over to owner Annie, she pulls the lure toward herself instead of moving it straight down, causing Diamond to stand. If you simply repeat your instructions over and over, Annie may become frustrated and Diamond's performance might start to deteriorate. So, explain things in a different way. Give Annie an image to visualize: "The motion you make with your hand should look like you're drawing the letter L." There, now Annie is more likely to make the luring motion correctly. If she still has difficulty with it, you could put your hand over hers (always ask before touching a client), then perform the luring motion so Diamond lays down. Do this a few times, then have Annie try it herself.

Another alternative would be to put Diamond in another room

altogether and have Annie practice without him. You can even hold a pillow or other object to mark where the dog's head would be. I'll admit I have even been known to play the dog so the owner can practice. When the dog returns, the owner can perform the lure correctly, and the dog's grasp of the behavior has not diminished in the meantime.

*Trainers First*

The way we train dogs and their people is a bit odd, if you think about it. First, we take a dog and person who have no knowledge of a specific skill, and teach it to each of them. We then turn the inexperienced dog over to the inexperienced person and expect the two novices to muddle through together. Strange, isn't it?

Lead a dog through at least a few repetitions of an exercise so he has a basic understanding of it before turning him over to the owner. Then, as the owner practices with the dog, offer constructive feedback. Make sure the owner feels confident enough with the exercise to continue working on it between sessions.

It is helpful for owners to understand how to train an exercise from beginning to end. But if the owner has physical limitations, poor coordination, poor timing, or the dog does not lure easily, it can sometimes help to get the dog further along in an exercise before turning him over to the owner. When Annie had trouble luring Diamond into a down, one solution was to improve her luring skills before allowing her to continue working with Diamond. An alternate solution would have been to get Diamond to the point where he would perform the down on a hand signal without the treat lure, and then turn him over to Annie. At that point Annie's job would have been to simply give the hand signal, making things easier for everybody.

How much progress a dog should make before he is turned over to his owner is a judgement call, based on your assessment of the skill levels of dog and owner. For many dogs, ensuring that the exercise has been performed smoothly a few times before the owner takes over is sufficient. In other cases, working with the dog more extensively first will help to ensure that even if the client performs the lure or signal slightly differently than you did, the dog will make the mental leap and perform the exercise correctly.

Do whatever is necessary to set both dog and owner up to succeed, and to ensure that the owner is able to successfully get the dog to perform the behavior before you end the session.

*Treating Your Clients Like Dogs*

There is an entire section on how to apply dog training skills to people in *It's Not the Dogs, It's the People*. To briefly reiterate the most important points:

- Set the stage for success by breaking exercises down into small, understandable pieces.
- Proceed gradually, building upon each success.
- Explain things simply and clearly. Analogies can be helpful.
- Leave the scientific jargon at home.
- Don't forget the positive reinforcement! Let clients know when they are doing a great job.
- Keep the momentum going during lessons. Being social is fine, but do less chatting and more training to ensure that lessons stay on track.

Once you have given clear instructions, offered feedback, answered questions and positively reinforced dog and owner, it is up to the client to follow through between sessions.

Coming up next, how to get that all-important client compliance!

# 18

# *Protocols and Suggestions*

You could design a perfectly brilliant protocol to solve a dog's problem, but if the client does not comply, the plan is worthless. When formulating plans and making suggestions, we trainers naturally take the dog's issues and temperament into account; but it is important to consider the client's personality and lifestyle as well.

*A Border Collie in Human Clothing?*

A meticulous, driven, goal-oriented human personality type is more likely to follow a detailed, step-by-step protocol than one who is more... scattered. Look for clues not only in what your clients *say* they are willing to do, but in what you observe. At the home of Wanda and her German Shepherd Tipper, you notice that her house has a "lived in" quality. Magazines, papers and the detritus of everyday life are strewn over every available surface. As you search for a place to set your things down, Wanda apologetically gathers kids' toys and assorted laundry items to clear a spot for you on the couch. It takes her five minutes to locate a paper and pen with which to take notes. Do you think Wanda has the time and inclination to follow a strict protocol that will require time, patience and meticulous attention to detail? The paper it's printed on would likely make a lovely coloring page for her three-year-old.

Recommendations should also be tailored to the information you gather during the history-taking process. When asked how many times a day Tipper is fed, Wanda replies that she leaves the food down all day, because it is convenient. When asked what type of exercise Tipper gets, she says, "Oh, she runs around in the back yard." When pressed as to whether anyone actually plays with Tipper in the yard or takes her for walks, Wanda responds that with the family's hectic schedule, no one really has the time. Again, a complicated, time-consuming program or one that requires major lifestyle changes is not likely to meet with success in this particular household.

Designing a protocol that will fit in with the time constraints and physical and energetic capabilities of each client will make your programs more likely to succeed. Some clients are wonderful at finding time to work with and exercise their dogs, no matter how busy they are. With others, you may have to make suggestions as to how to fit the program into their lifestyle. One family's solution could involve the wife taking the dog for a brisk walk in the morning before work, the adolescent son playing with the dog in the yard after school, and the husband walking the dog when he returns from work. The few brief daily training sessions could be a shared responsibility. As a general rule, for families who have limited time, are not willing or able to follow complicated protocols, or need the problem fixed yesterday, simpler is better.

Remember too that some clients, by the time they have called you, are at the end of the proverbial rope and need to see immediate results. While you must offer enough of a structured plan to make headway, a combination of management to improve the situation immediately and simple exercises to work toward a goal has the greatest chance of meeting with compliance, and therefore success.

### The Art of Compromise

Here is a case from my own files that illustrates the value of compromise: Irene, a feisty forty-something redhead, and her equally feisty Lhasa Apso, Toby, had a problem. Toby lunged and barked at other dogs during walks. Irene normally walked Toby on a retractable leash and flat buckle collar. When I advised her to use a standard (non-retractable) leash instead, she balked. Irene explained that Toby enjoyed being able to wander back and forth in front of her, sniffing the grass on either side of the walkway. Besides, she never encountered dogs during their mid-day walk, as no one on her long cul-de-sac owned a dog. But Irene also took Toby for evening walks on the paseos, a network of narrow pathways that winds through the city—a popular spot with dog owners. After patiently listening to me explain the training and safety reasons for keeping Toby close by means of a standard leash, Irene protested that she did not want to give up the retractable leash.

After some discussion, we reached a compromise. Irene would continue to use the retractable leash on mid-day walks on her own street, keeping a watchful eye for other dogs just in case. For her evening strolls on the paseos, she would use the standard leash. Why did I compromise? First, Irene was right in that she was unlikely to encounter other dogs on her cul-de-sac, especially mid-day. Also, I knew that insisting Irene give up the retractable leash entirely was not going to work, and might cause resentment. While it is important to the success of your training programs that clients comply with your suggestions, know your clients and pick your battles. In Irene's case, had I pressed the issue, she very likely would have used the leash she preferred anyway, and would have been less inclined to comply with further suggestions. Besides, by your demonstrating and her using the standard leash some of the time, Irene might come to realize how much easier it is to work with and eventually abandon the retractable leash on her own.

If a client seems resistant to a suggestion, try to pin down what part of the suggestion is troublesome. It may be that the whole concept is alien. For example, crate training is something with which many owners are not familiar. If unfamiliarity is the reason, explain why and how the proposed solution works and how it would be beneficial in that particular situation. If the objection involves the frequency or intensity of effort required, consider whether, within reason, adjustments can be made.

There are some instructions that should not be negotiable. Although your clients might believe it is perfectly reasonable to expect their five-month-old Labrador Retriever pup to stay on the front lawn alone off-leash, you know better. Put your foot down and explain why that expectation would be not only unrealistic, but potentially hazardous to the pup's well-being.

If clients are continually dismissive of your suggestions or argumentative, gently remind them that you are the expert for whose time and expertise they are paying. You do not need to blurt, "Look lady, I don't know why you paid me to come out here if you're not going to take any of my suggestions"—even if it is what you are thinking. A better approach would be to say kindly but firmly, "I've worked with this issue quite extensively over the years and I can assure you that this approach works. Why don't you try it for the next two weeks, and we'll take it from there." This authoritative yet polite approach will prevent clients from feeling they have been strong-armed, which will in turn improve the likelihood of compliance.

*Don't Pull the Rug Out…*

King, a two-year-old Jack Russell Terrier, has shown aggression toward family members. King snapped at Lisa recently when she tried to move him off the bed, and has growled at both Lisa and her husband Dan on numerous occasions, when they attempted to take bones or toys from him. There have been other challenges as well. Lisa now jokingly refers to King as their Jack Russell Terrorist, but truth be told, she is becoming nervous around him and is worried that his behavior is getting progressively worse.

After taking a thorough history and assessing King's behavior, you decide that King would benefit from a leadership, or "learn to earn" program, among other things. Since the program's success will depend on the compliance of King's owners, you must be careful not to overwhelm them by suggesting too many changes at once. If you recommend that King sleep on the floor instead of the bed, be ignored when he demonstrates pushy, attention-seeking behavior, and must sit before meals, petting and tosses of the ball, Dan and Lisa should not feel overwhelmed. These small changes can easily be incorporated into their lifestyle and will soon become habit. However, instructing the couple to implement those changes *and* to stop allowing King on the furniture, pet him only as a reward for performing a requested behavior, walk him three times daily, and follow an intricate resource-guarding protocol might be asking too much at once. It might even cause Dan and Lisa to consider other options for King's future, since his rehabilitation seems such an enormous undertaking. The moral? As effective as a program might be, if your clients feel too overwhelmed to follow through, it is useless. That, and be careful what you name your dog!

*Go Slow with Canine Changes*

Imagine the reaction of a teenager if she were informed that a 9 p.m. curfew is now in effect, that she is no longer allowed to go out without permission, and that she must submit a daily report as to how her allowance is being spent. Trust me, it wouldn't be pretty. Rebellion can result when too many restrictions are applied at once—and that response is not limited to humans. Be careful not to suggest so many changes to a dog's lifestyle that your clients end up with the canine equivalent of a teenage rebellion. This concept is especially important when working with dogs with aggression issues, since the goal is to keep the dog calm, not stress him out.

> *A little at a time is effective and kind!*

*Be Specific*

Wouldn't it be nice if you could just swing a dog bone back and forth like a pendulum while intoning, "You weeell followww my suggessstions..."? Since hypnotizing clients might be frowned upon by the authorities, do the next best thing; make training easy by making your suggestions as specific as possible. Sit down with your client and make a list of what her dog finds rewarding. Ask specific questions: Does he like going for a walk? Chasing a ball? Being petted? Playing with other dogs? Once you have figured out what the dog likes, help your client find ways to fit those real-life rewards into daily training. For example, to encourage calm behavior, your client could pet her dog each time he lies on his dog bed. Access to other dogs could be used as a reward by requiring her dog to walk nicely next to her until they reach the other dogs.

Many owners still believe training practice involves long, boring drills—a prospect about which most people are, understandably, not thrilled. But even if lengthy, repetitive sessions *were* the best way to train (they're not—dogs learn better in short sessions), nowadays very few people have much free time. Most modern trainers advise multiple, brief training sessions throughout the day. Three to five practice sessions of three to five minutes apiece is plenty, along with incorporating the behaviors into everyday life.

Help clients find creative ways to fit short training sessions into their day. For example, Sheila has mentioned that most evenings, her family gathers in the living room to watch television. So you suggest they practice down-stays with Shotzie during commercial breaks. Sheila has purchased the training treats you recommend. Since they come in a sausage-like roll, you suggest that while Sheila is cutting the roll into treat-sized pieces, Shotzie should remain in a down-stay. Sheila is to toss small pieces to Shotzie for staying in place, in rapid succession at first and then gradually lengthening the time between tosses. Since these suggestions are specific and easy to follow, Sheila is likely to comply.

Posting a checklist on the refrigerator can be helpful for some clients, to remind them of what needs to be done each day. Or, families can assign tasks such as walking the dog, then designate on a calendar who is responsible for which training chore each day. Whatever system works for the client is fine, but be sure there is a specific plan in place before you leave.

# Part VI

## *Questions, Answers and Other Helpful Stuff*

# 19

# *Commonly Asked Questions*

In discussions with other trainers in person and online, certain questions have cropped up over and over. Since these are obviously areas of concern to many trainers, some of the most frequently asked questions have been included here. You will also find questions on topics you might never have considered, discussions of issues you may find uncomfortable, and tips on ways to handle awkward situations.

*How do I know when my work with a client is finished?*

The obvious answer would be, "When the dog is trained, of course!" If you were direct with your client at the beginning of your training relationship, it should be clear when that goal has been reached. Perhaps you sold three sessions with the agreement that the dog would understand eight pre-determined cues by the completion of training, but that it would be up to the client to continue improving the dog's skills. Or maybe you sold ten sessions with the understanding that by completion the dog would perform the learned behaviors reliably, even in the presence of distractions. Either way, if you pre-sold a specified number of sessions and clarified what would be accomplished in those sessions, the completion date would be obvious.

But things are not always so clear-cut. If you see clients session by session, it can sometimes be difficult to determine when to end the training relationship. Setting clear goals, and periodically reviewing with clients what has been accomplished and what has yet to be addressed, can ease this confusion. If you simply turn up session after session without a plan and ask the client what she wants to work on, it will be difficult to know when training should be terminated.

I have had some clients who, although training goals had been reached, wanted to continue. They enjoyed the training, and the weekly lessons motivated them to continue working with the dog. In those cases I was careful to clarify that although initial goals had been reached, I would be happy to continue so long as training continued to be productive. I have heard of trainers who string clients along session after session, coming up with new behaviors the dog suddenly "must" learn. If you feel there is nothing more to be covered with a particular owner-dog team, say so. If there are further skills you feel would be beneficial, train on!

*Should I barter for my services?*

Bartering means exchanging goods or services. Whether you should barter your training services depends on the situation and on how well you know the client. I know a trainer who bartered her services for a set of living room curtains. That might sound odd, but her client was a gifted seamstress. The trainer couldn't wait for these lovely creations to grace her living room. Long after the agreed-upon three training sessions had been completed, the woman was still working on the curtains. Although the trainer eventually received the finished product, it took much longer than expected and caused friction in their relationship.

I do not barter, but I know many trainers who do. I know one trainer who trades training sessions for massage sessions. I can definitely see the appeal! Another exchanges training for pet sitting services. If you choose to barter, no matter how well you know the person, create a contract. Outline specifically what is to be exchanged, and within what time frame. A signed contract will encourage both parties to stick to the agreement and serve as evidence, should the deal be broken.

*What should I do if a dog bites me at a training session?*

Early in my training career I had an appointment with a client named John. John's initial complaint was that his three-year-old, 100-plus pound Rhodesian Ridgeback, Magda, was destructive. I arrived at the house just as John pulled into the driveway. We walked inside together, and John went to let Magda in from the back yard. As I stood in the narrow kitchen, a big, brown tank of a girl approached, wagging her tail happily. She appeared relaxed and friendly, and allowed me to pet her. Imagine my surprise when, after a few brief seconds of petting, Magda whipped around and sunk her canines into my forearm.

Magda had bitten once and released, but wore a look that said in no uncertain terms that she was considering a repeat performance. Fortunately, I tend to remain perfectly calm during a crisis, and fall apart later. I calmly asked John to put Magda outside. Since John was standing motionless with his jaw hanging open, this request had to be repeated, with increasing urgency. (If you find yourself faced with a CTZ—Client Turned Zombie—use his name to get his attention.) Once Magda was outside, we stood at the kitchen sink and poured hydrogen peroxide over my wound. It was not a very deep puncture nor was the pain intense; what was truly awful was the embarrassment I felt— me, a professional, getting bit!

I was in over my head; I had not had much experience with aggressive behavior at the time. I had, however, had years of experience with wolves and wolfdogs, and was adept at controlling my own body language and reading canine body language. I couldn't understand it. Had Magda bitten because I had touched a painful area on her body? No, I had been petting her in the same spot all along. Had I been leaning over her? No. Made a sudden movement? No. I felt foolish and confused.

John and I sat down to talk, and it was eventually revealed that Magda had tried to bite five other people—all with no apparent warning. Also, she had been on a medication for the past year that has a known side effect of increasing aggressive behavior in a small percentage of dogs. Oh, and she was coming into heat! I believe that was the exact moment I created the mental file labeled "Things That Are Good to Know." I explained to John that his plan to breed Magda was ill-advised, and recommended a veterinary exam, including a full thyroid panel (there is a link between thyroid dysfunction and aggression). After discussing liability, the importance of management, and more, I referred John to another trainer. Unpleasant as the whole experience was, I learned a lot from it, including the importance of asking very specific questions on the phone before the appointment.

No matter how careful you are, if you train dogs long enough, odds are that some day you will be bitten. If you are bitten during a training session, remain calm. In most cases, a bite will be just that—a single bite, or at worst, a rapid series of bites, after which the dog will back off. In either case, do not yell or act aggressively toward the dog; doing so could escalate the behavior. If the owner is nearby and you feel she is capable, calmly ask her to move the dog out of the area or to put him on leash. It is best if the owner remains calm as well, since an overly-excited human can easily make an already reactive dog more so.

Once the dog is safely contained, treat the wound if necessary, then sit down with the owner. Although you might be upset, retain a professional demeanor. Explain what happened. If the bite was exacerbated by something the owner did, explain neutrally why it happened, so that it does not happen again. If something you did contributed to the bite, chalk it up as a learning experience. Then discuss your recommendations or refer the case to another trainer.

If you arrange your introductions carefully and are aware of and respect canine body language, it is unlikely that you will end up on the receiving end of a flat-out, non-stop attack. If the worst happens, do whatever it takes to defend yourself while doing the least possible damage to the dog. Some dogs will back off from a loud verbal assault. If necessary, grab a solid object and place it between you and the dog—your notebook might come in handy in this regard. Or, stuff something (other than a body part) in his mouth. If possible, engage the owner's help. Get the dog safely contained in a room, crate or outdoors as quickly as possible.

Depending on the state in which you live, you might be required to report a bite to the authorities. The owner will be asked to produce the dog's medical records, to ensure against the possibility of rabies. If the owner cannot provide those records, you may be required to get a series of rabies shots just in case. Despite the fact that *you* will not press charges, impress upon the owners that should someone else be on the receiving end of a bite, that person might well pursue legal action. Tell owners in no uncertain terms that should they be sued, they could lose assets including their home and/or homeowners insurance, and their dog would likely end up euthanized.

Above all, if you are bitten, try not to let it shake your confidence. Some of the best trainers I know have been bitten more than once. You cannot control all circumstances, environments, clients or dogs. Pay careful attention to canine body language and stress levels, and if you feel a situation is becoming dangerous, speak up before it escalates.

*Should I expect clients to provide training treats?*

Bring a variety of training treats to your first session with new clients. Many owners are unaware that training treats should be small and easily chewed, so they might not have appropriate treats on hand. By carrying various types of treats, you are likely to find one the dog likes. You can then recommend the client purchase the product (either through you or at a store) to be used at future sessions. Take treats with you to *all* sessions in case clients forget or have run out.

*What if my client is not working with the dog or following my suggestions?*

In *Protocols and Suggestions,* strategies were offered to promote client compliance. If you have tried those tactics and your client still does not follow your suggestions, it is time to offer a choice. For example, Pam refuses to crate train her ten-week old Labrador Retriever puppy. Despite your explanations, Pam feels that "putting Sage in a box" is inhumane. Instead of insisting that Pam do something to which she is so opposed, offer a few options and ask her to choose one. Sage could be leashed to Pam, following everywhere she goes; he could be tethered to a piece of furniture wherever Pam is spending time; or he could be left in a puppy pen, back yard, or gated-off kitchen. Giving the owner a choice empowers her, but it also puts the onus on her to take responsibility for the choice she makes.

In the case of practicing obedience exercises, compliance could be due to a lack of time on the client's part. Help your client find ways to incorporate training into her schedule. Perhaps she could have the dog go to bed and down-stay each day during breakfast; when playing fetch, the dog could be required to perform an exercise before each toss of the ball. Be creative. Once solutions have been agreed upon, tell your client that you will be checking on the dog's progress at the next appointment. For many people, knowing a "show and tell" will be expected is sufficient incentive to work with the dog between sessions.

I know a trainer whose rule of thumb is "never work harder than the owner"—and she's right. If despite your best efforts, an owner continually neglects to practice between sessions, you are wasting your time. There is nothing more frustrating than arriving at a client's home week after week only to hear, "I didn't have time to work with the dog." This scenario not only negates any chance of making progress, but could seem a poor reflection on you when that person tells others you trained the dog.

If you find yourself with an incompliant client, be firm and direct. Explain that although you would like to continue training, that will be impossible unless you arrive at the next session to see that progress has been made. That might not be an easy thing to say, but it will save you a lot of frustration in the long run. If your client has pre-paid a number of sessions, you are bound by contract to finish them; but if the client is on a single-session plan, tell her to call to schedule another session once she has found time to work with the dog.

Over time, you will learn to recognize and weed out unmotivated types during the initial phone inquiry, so you will have to deal with this situation less frequently. Just be sure to explain to callers before you ever set up a session that you are really training them to train their dog, and that they will be expected to work with the dog between sessions.

*When training obedience exercises, should the dog be on-leash or off?*

When working outdoors, unless you have a safe, enclosed training space, the dog should always be on leash for safety reasons. For distance work, a long line should be used. When working indoors, if you use a training method that involves leash corrections (which I do not use nor recommend), the dog would obviously have to be leashed. Since I use reward-based methods that do not include leash corrections, I prefer the dog be off-leash for the majority of indoor training. After all, when the owner gives the dog a cue in the house, the dog will not normally be leashed.

To teach basic obedience exercises, I almost never touch dogs (except possibly to pet, as part of the reward). Since I prefer instead to lure or shape them into position, a leash is unnecessary. However, one circumstance that would warrant a leash indoors would be when working with a dog who continually runs off, plays around, jumps up, or is otherwise difficult to manage. But even then, you do not have to actually hold the leash for all exercises. You could either stand on the leash or tether the dog to a piece of furniture. That way your hands are free but the dog is still managed. If it is your preference that dogs be leashed for indoor training, you could start on-leash and progress to off-leash indoor practice.

*How do I make a recommendation for euthanasia?*

I have worked with dogs who had inflicted multiple puncture-wounds on multiple people, yet I felt the dogs were workable. I have seen others who, although they had not yet inflicted serious bites, made the hairs on my neck stand on end. If you work with aggressive dogs long enough, you will develop a gut instinct about which dogs are truly dangerous, and unfortunately, will probably come across a few for whom you would recommend euthanasia. There are not many options for a dog who has bitten repeatedly, severely or unpredictably, or who has mauled someone—especially a child.

Assuming you have exhausted all possible solutions, including behavior modification (with or without medication), rehoming and rescue, it is time to have a serious discussion with your client. Be direct but compassionate. Open with a statement such as, "I know this must be terribly difficult for you." There is nothing wrong with letting clients know this is difficult for you as well. Review the options. Explain that at this point, the dog is beyond behavior modification, with or without medication. Stress the potential liability that could be involved, should the dog bite again. Being sued could mean the loss of the home along with the possibility of future homeowners insurance, and the dog would likely lose his life. Explain why rehoming is not an option, since no one wants a dog with a known aggression issue (plus there could be liability involved should the dog bite again). Some people believe that giving the dog to a rescue group is an option. Explain that most rescue groups will not take in dogs with severe aggression issues, since they are not adoptable.

If the client wishes to keep the dog, management is the only option. Explain in detail what specific measures would be required to keep everyone safe, and that these measures would be necessary for the rest of the dog's life. If there are children involved, the chances of 100% solid, reliable management is almost nil. In that case, a pen or enclosure could be built, with a perimeter fence around it and a padlock. It might be necessary that the children no longer have any interaction with the dog. Does that sound harsh? Of course. But the client cannot be allowed to let things remain as they are, hoping there will be no further incidents. Impress upon owners exactly how much time and effort management would entail, and ask them to consider what the dog's quality of life would be like.

Since the dog can not be rehabilitated, rescued or rehomed, unless the owner chooses to manage the dog for life, the only alternative left is euthanasia. Although in rare, extreme circumstances you might directly recommend euthanasia, in most cases owners should be the ones to make the decision. Most owners will come to this conclusion without you having to spell it out. In some cases, the owner already knows deep down that euthanasia is the only possible option, but needs your confirmation and support.

During this conversation, people will become emotional. Obviously, this is one of the most difficult decisions a dog owner could ever face. Some people feel overwhelming guilt that they have somehow failed the dog. The best thing you can do is be supportive and listen, and let owners know this is not their fault. If you are aware of resources such as cremation services or grief counseling, pass the information along. If you are willing, you could even offer to accompany owners to the vet's office for the euthanasia. Personally, I have a difficult time with this emotionally so I do not make the offer, but I know trainers who do so regularly. And if I had a client who really needed me to be there, despite my reservations, I would go.

Follow up by writing a letter to the client's vet, explaining the case and why you have recommended euthanasia. It is a kind gesture to send a sympathy card to the client and to follow up by phone a few weeks later. Be aware that emotionally difficult cases take a toll not only on owners, but on trainers as well. Monitor your own stress levels and when things get overwhelming, take a break or do something nice for yourself. Prevent burnout so you are emotionally fit to help future clients.

*Should I offer free evaluations?*

This is a matter of personal preference. I do not offer free evaluations. I spend valuable time traveling to and from clients' homes and assessing situations, for which I expect to be paid. Besides, my first session combines evaluating *and* working with the dog, which is definitely not free. One possible reason to offer free evaluations early in your career would be because you do not yet have a lot of experience and are uncertain as to whether you will want to take on a specific case. A free evaluation allows you to assess a situation before you commit to working with the dog. Should you decline, the client is not out fees and you can feel comfortable referring the case.

Some experienced trainers use the free evaluation as a marketing tool. The potential client has nothing to lose, and might well choose that trainer over one who expects a large sum up front for a package of sessions. Free evaluations may be done in person, and if the trainer is a good salesperson and sells large packages of sessions, doing "free" evaluations can be well worth her time. Some trainers offer free evaluations by phone. The evaluation might be similar to the initial intake conversation many trainers have anyway, or it could be more in-depth and time-consuming.

Keep the free evaluation in mind as a marketing tool, but be careful that you do not give away your valuable time truly free of charge.

*What about doing free work or offering reduced rates?*

Although I regularly offer discounted training to those who have adopted from shelter and rescue organizations, I rarely do so otherwise. You might think that uncaring; it's not. I have learned the hard way that free or deeply discounted training is almost never effective. Many people do not value things that are obtained cheaply or free of charge, so there is little motivation to follow through with training. Some people simply love a bargain and will try to haggle. Never negotiate your rates! It is unprofessional and besides, someone who haggles over your rates is also likely to haggle over suggestions you make during the training process.

If you are approached by a dog owner who is truly in need and you would like to help, begin by quoting whatever discounted rate you feel comfortable with, rather than bargaining your way down. Or, if your first session is normally an hour and a half, offer to do an hour instead at your normal rate. If your rates are still too high, refer to another trainer whose rates are lower or to a group class, where the same amount of money will buy more sessions.

*What if I truly dislike a client and do not want to return?*

Fortunately, most people you work with will be pleasant, and even the ones you don't love will be tolerable. However, there is bound to be a client or two to whose home you do not wish to return. Maybe the person made improper comments, was completely obnoxious or downright nasty. Whatever the case, the nice thing about this business is, you don't have to ever see the person again!

One way to prevent getting "stuck" with a client you don't want is to sell single sessions, or to hold off on offering a package of sessions until after the first session has been completed. By offering single sessions there is no obligation for the client or you to continue the relationship. If you choose not to offer a package deal at the end of the first session, you are not legally bound to return.

Although you could tell a client point-blank why you are no longer interested in working with her, such a direct statement can be difficult. It is rare that I do not wish to continue working with a client, but if it happens, I might end the session by saying, "Why don't you work with the dog for a few weeks, then give me a call to schedule the next appointment." Don't get me wrong—I say the same thing to some clients with behavior cases and mean it, and we follow through. But whether it is due to a lack of rapport or because the person senses a hesitance on my part, those I do not wish to continue working with do not normally call back. And if they do, I can always find an excuse to discontinue the training. Again, this sort of thing is rare, but it is good to be prepared in case it does happen.

*How do I work with two dogs in a home?*

One word: *separately*. The easiest and most productive way to train two dogs is to work with one at a time. Advise your client in advance to have a chew bone or stuffed Kong™ prepared so one dog can happily chew away in another room while you work with the other one. Even though you will explain, demonstrate, practice, and then have the client practice each exercise with the first dog, it is important that you both work with the second dog as well. Leaving your client with the advice, "Practice later with your other dog" is asking for trouble, since the second dog might not respond in the same way as the first. Walk the client and second dog through each exercise so you can make modifications if necessary.

Explain to your client how to practice with each dog separately on her own. She could practice with one dog while the other was in another room, or tethered or crated in the training area. Or, if the dogs have a solid down-stay, one dog could remain in a down-stay while the other works, with the client periodically tossing treats to the down-staying dog.

Once both dogs are proficient at an exercise, work with them together. Keep in mind that in each other's presence, the dogs' behavior will not be as reliable. You can make things easier at first by lowering your criteria—for example, not expecting lighting-fast downs, or luring the first few repetitions of an exercise. It can also be helpful to work the dogs at a distance from each other at first, bringing them closer together as they perform successfully.

At first, you and the client should each handle one dog. Progress to your handling both dogs at once, explaining what you are doing as you go. For example, if one dog breaks the down-stay, you might say, "Notice that as I moved toward Buddy to get him back into a down-stay, I reminded Buster to stay by giving the hand signal." Be sure to have the client practice with both dogs during your lesson, so you can give feedback and she can be more effective when practicing on her own.

*What should I do if my client and I encounter a stray dog during a training session?*

This has happened to me a few times. I now tell clients at the beginning of any outdoor training session that if we encounter a stray dog and I have their dog's leash at the time, I will quickly hand their dog over so that I can intercept the stray. Or, if the client's dog is small, the client should quickly pick the dog up on my verbal signal. If you work in areas that are known to have stray dogs, practice this with clients outdoors by suddenly saying, "Take your dog!" That way if the real thing happens, the owner has had practice and is less likely to become a CTZ (Client Turned Zombie) while you attempt to deal with two out-of-control dogs.

What happens next depends on the stray. With some, it is enough to stand in front of your client and her dog and sternly tell the stray to, "Go home!" This can be accompanied by an authoritative wave of the arm. Whether you should attempt this is a judgement call that depends on the stray's demeanor and your gut feeling. You do not want to endanger anyone by escalating the arousal level of a dog who is already reactive. One alternative that has a lower chance of increasing the arousal level of the stray is to toss a shower of treats on the ground, and then walk your client and her dog quickly in the opposite direction.

Again, how you should react depends on the situation—an extreme case might require an extreme response. Once, at a local park, I body-tackled a pair of small dogs who were making an aggressive beeline for my client's dog, who most definitely would have had them for hors d'ouevres. My client's dog was large and not easy to pick up, and my client had gone CTZ. In that particular case, other than my getting scraped up, everything worked out fine. But I do not recommend physically engaging strays, as doing so puts one at risk for redirected aggression.

Safety precautions might include carrying an airhorn—a cannister with a horn on top that blares at an incredibly loud volume. Airhorns can be obtained at boating supply stores and have been effective in breaking up many a dogfight. Another item that is easily carried is Direct Stop™, a cannister that resembles a can of pepper spray, but instead sprays citronella. (See *Resources.*) The spray is most effective when used *before* dogs have reached the point of actual physical engagement. Of course, the best defense is a good offense—always be aware of your surroundings.

*What can I do about clients who are not authoritative or consistent enough with their dogs?*

This scenario is all too common. Trainers are often called in to deal with jumping, mouthing and other "manners" type problems. This is especially common in adolescent, high-energy dogs. If *owners* can be trained to implement a leadership program (together with providing plenty of exercise and mental stimulation), often the dog's behavior improves dramatically. The problem comes when a client is extremely "soft," i.e., coos constantly at the dog, repeats cues over and over, and generally lets the dog do what he likes. Often the children in these homes have behavior issues as well.

You are not going to change someone's personality. Rather than insisting that an owner develop a strong, confident demeanor, find ways she can effectively enforce leadership. For example, even the mousiest of owners can switch a dog from being free-fed to eating twice daily, and ask for sits before meals. (If the leadership program needs a jump-start, have the owner hand-feed meals for two weeks.) Anyone is capable of asking a dog to sit before receiving rewards such as going for a walk or chasing a ball. Find things your client *can* do.

Offer information on both canine and human body language, teach hand signals, and stress habits such as having the dog's attention before giving cues. Explain why complying whenever the dog wants something (e.g., throwing the ball because the dog has dropped it at one's feet) is a bad idea. Instruct clients to either have the dog do something before giving him what he wants, or to simply ignore him. Demonstrate simple solutions that do not require force, such as turning to the side and ignoring when the dog jumps (then rewarding for sitting or having four paws on the ground). Have the client practice these skills, and offer feedback. Once your clients see how successful these simple tactics can be, they will be more likely to implement them in everyday life. Remember, you can't change the person, but you can offer all the appropriate tools to achieve success.

That said, you will encounter some people who are not unable, but are simply unwilling to do anything they perceive as being remotely unpleasant for the dog. For example, some owners refuse to manage or contain a dog in any way, saying, "Oh, but he'd hate being in that little crate" or, "I don't want to break his spirit!" There is something to be said for compromise and finding solutions that work for everyone, but at some point a line is crossed and you are working harder than the owner. As previously mentioned, that is not acceptable. Explain and make suggestions, and give owners every opportunity to achieve success. But know when to put your foot down and assert that if clients are not willing to accept your suggestions, the dog's behavior is not going to improve and you will not continue to work with them.

*Any tips for working with elderly clients?*

There are aspects of working with the elderly that frustrate some trainers. Some geriatric owners have trouble remembering instructions; some have limited mobility; others have diminished mental acuity. This is not to suggest that every elderly person is impaired in some way. My parents are in their late seventies/early eighties and are sharp mentally and fit physically. In fact, my mother can swim laps around me! Be kind and patient, and do not patronize the elderly. With any luck, you will join their ranks someday.

When designing training exercises and solutions to behavior problems, take into account your client's range of motion and any physical limitations. I had an elderly client who loved the Halti™ head halter since it made her dog so much easier to walk, but she lacked sufficient tensile strength to squeeze the plastic quick-release device. Fortunately, the Gentle Leader™ worked just as well and she was able to manipulate its quick-release with ease. Had that solution not worked, another possibility would have been to remove the quick-release tab and sew velcro in its place. Or, we might have gone to a different type of training device altogether.

Find something your client *can* do and give specific instructions on how to practice with the dog. For example, to teach "go to bed," your client could simply sit on the couch and toss the dog a treat each time he goes to the bed on his own. I once attended a seminar given by a clicker trainer who was in a wheelchair—she was one of the best clicker trainers I have seen. Limitations are only limitations if you lack creativity.

When working with clients who have physical limitations, it helps to be familiar with local resources and various products. An owner who cannot physically walk the dog might be willing to hire a dog-walker, or to send the dog to doggie daycare a few times a week. If the dog is small, you could suggest a toy such as the previously mentioned Chase N' Pull Tug Toy™ (see *Resources*), which does not require much exertion or mobility on the part of the owner. Teaching a retrieve is another good way to exercise a dog without exercising the owner.

Be sure to take mental and energetic capabilities into account. Do not expect someone with a memory and/or attention deficit to follow a lengthy or complicated protocol. Pare things down to the essentials. Repeat information as necessary and be sure the person takes notes or is left with printed instructions. Use management whenever possible so the dog's behavior can improve immediately, with little effort on the part of the owner. The more creative your solutions and the more attention you pay to the needs of the person as well as those of the dog, the more effective you will be in working with elderly clients.

## 20

# *Endnote*

On the pages that follow you will find compilations of information:

The *Resources* section lists products and services that have been mentioned.

*Appendix A* contains forms and contracts. Feel free to use them as is or amend as needed. This section also contains handouts that may be given to your clients.

*Appendix B* contains questionnaires from the history-taking section, condensed for ease of reproduction and use at training sessions.

*Appendix C* lists schools, books and other resources with which to further your education.

Education is an ongoing process. No matter how experienced and knowledgeable you become, keep reading, attending seminars, and networking with other trainers. Once you have become an accomplished in-home trainer yourself, help and mentor those who are just starting their careers.

I hope that you have found this book helpful, and wish you all the best in your training career.

*Nicole Wilde*

# Resources

## Booklets (Client Handouts)

*The Cautious Canine*
Patricia B. McConnell, Ph.D.
Black Earth, WI: Dog's Best Friend, Ltd. 1998 ISBN 1-891767-00-3

*Leader of the Pack*
Patricia B. McConnell, Ph.D.
Black Earth, WI: Dog's Best Friend, Ltd. 1996 ISBN 1-891767-02-X

Patricia McConnell's books are available in bulk through
www.dogsbestfriendtraining.com

*Taking Care of Puppy Business*
Gail Pivar and Leslie Nelson
South Elgin, IL: Tails-U-Win! Inc., 1998 ISBN0-9710084-1-8
(Available in bulk through www.tailsuwin.com.
See site for other booklets.)
860-646-5033

## Products

**Assess-A-Hand**
(also Sue Sternberg videos)
www.suesternberg.com

**Chase N' Pull Tug Toy™**
Dogwise
www.dogwise.com
1-800-776-2665

**Clickers (imprinted)**

| | | |
|---|---|---|
| SitStay.com | and | The Clicker Company |
| 1-800-SIT-STAY | | 480-706-1884 |
| www.sitstay.com | | www.clickercompany.com |

**Gentle Leaders™, Martingales, Leashes, Direct Stop™, more.**
Premier Pet Products  (Trainers may set up account/purchase in bulk.)
406 Branchway Road
Richmond, VA 23236
1-800-933-5595
www.premier.com

**K9 Cruiser**
V-Tag
www.v-tag.com/k9cruise.htm

**Kong™ products** (discounted to trainers—resale program)
ProActive Pet Products
510-420-8070
www.proactivepet.com

**Muzzles**
Morrco Pet Supply
1-800-575-1451
www.morrco.com

**Refrigerator Magnets** (personalized)
www.kissmfg.com

**Tethers**

Pat Miller
www.peaceablepaws.com

Paul Owens
www.raisewithpraise.com
1-800-269-3591

# Catalogs

These catalogs have reasonable prices, especially when buying in bulk. Some carry specialized equipment such as kevlar gloves, muzzles, etc.

Care-A-Lot Pet Supply Warehouse
1-800-343-7680
www.carealotpets.com

JB Wholesale Pet Supplics, Inc.
1-800-526-0388
www.jbpet.com

KV Vet Supply
1-800-423-8211
www.kvvet.com

Pet Edge (formerly New England Serum)
1-800-738-3343
www.petedge.com

Ryan's Pet Supplies (wholesale pet care products)
1-800-525-7387
www.RyansPet.com

# Association of Pet Dog Trainers (APDT)
P.O. Box 1781
Hobbs, NM 88241
1-800-PET-DOGS
www.apdt.com

# CPDT Exam

Certification Council for Pet Dog Trainers
ccpdt.org
203-847-4766

# Liability Insurance

Business Insurers of the Carolinas
P.O. Box 2536
Chapel Hill, NC 27515-2536
800-962-4611

Mourer-Foster, Inc.
The Hartford
800-686-2663

# Appendix A

# Forms, Contracts
# and Handouts

# Appendix A

Intake Form
Contract: Package Deal
Contract: Single Session
Handout: Positive Training Principles & Tips
Handout: Leadership
Handout: Introduction to Clicker Training
Handout: Crate Training

Note: Intake form and contracts may be reproduced and used with your own company name and logo added. Be sure to have an attorney review contracts before use, to ensure their validity in your state.

Handouts may be reproduced with your company name and logo as well, but must be printed with copyright line intact.

Name _____ Date _____

Address _____ Dog _____

Phone _____ Breed _____

E-mail _____ Age/Sex _____

Ref. by _____ Neut.? _____

Other Pets in Household _____

Other People in Household _____

Occupation/Time spent outside home _____

Veterinarian _____

Medical Problems/Allergies _____

Brand of Food _____ Times Fed _____

Eat immed./finish all? _____ Bones/Chewies _____

Other treats/snacks _____

Where/when dog was obtained _____

Housebroken? _____ Crate trained? _____ Sleep area _____

% indoors/outdoors _____ Where kept when owner gone _____

_____

Previous training: Cues/methods used/who trained _____

_____

Exercise Type/Frequency _____

_____

Has dog ever bitten or injured a person or animal? If so, describe: _____

_____

_____

Reason for Consultation: _____

_____

_____

_____

Notes: _____

_____

_____

_____

# TRAINING SERVICES AGREEMENT

I/We _____ (hereinafter referred to as "Client") have voluntarily employed _____ (herein after referred to as "Consultant") to assist me in the training of my dog(s) _____ .

**Professional Fees:**
Professional fees shall be $_____ for a series of _____ sessions, the first of which will be _____ hours, then _____ hour(s) for each remaining visit. "No shows" or cancelled appointments with less than 24 hours notice will be counted as one session. All sessions must be completed within _____ from the date of this contract. Any sessions not completed within that time frame will be forfeited.

**Desciption of Services:**
I understand that the Consultant will work directly with me and my pet to impart contemporary animal behavior knowledge that best fits our needs, and that successful companion pet programs depend on a combination of learned skills on the part of the pet and owner. Behavior is not static; an animal will not continue to perform even trained behaviors without ongoing practice. Especially in cases involving any type of aggression, although behavior may be modified, the dog is never considered "cured." A pet's behavior is ultimately the owner's responsibility. Consultant will make every reasonable effort to help us attain goals but makes no guarantees of performance on the part of Client or pet as a result of providing professional animal behavior consultation.

Client acknowledges that obedience training/behavior modification may be an activity in which damage or injury to dog(s) and/or persons may occur. Client will assume full financial/moral responsibility for the actions of their dog(s). Client further acknowledges that dog(s) may be exposed to a variety of environmental conditions which include, but are not limited to, vehicular travel, interaction with people and other animals, exposure to adverse weather, and exposure to areas with crowds and all types of traffic.

I/We Client agree that I, my/our heirs, assignees and legal representatives will not make claim against, sue, or attach the property of Consultant, her family, acquaintances, or any other person acting on her behalf (herein referred to as "Her Agents"), for injury or damage done to or by dog(s) resulting from action or negligence, however caused, by Consultant or Her Agents. I/We Client forever release Consultant and/or Her Agents from any and all liability and demands which I/We Client, and my/our heirs, assignees and legal representatives may have or may hereafter have for injury or damage to or by dog(s), and assume all risks thereof.

Client and Consultant hereby agree to mediate and/or arbitrate any misunderstanding that may arise pursuant to the terms contained herein. In any action or proceeding arising out of this agreement, the prevailing party shall be entitled to reimbursement of costs and legal fees.

This Contract for Training Services supersedes all other agreements, written or oral, previously made between Client and Consultant.

Executed on this _____ day of _____, 2_____

        "Client"                                 "Consultant"

_____     _____
        (print name)

_____
        (signature)

# TRAINING SERVICES AGREEMENT

I/We _____ (hereinafter referred to as "Client") have voluntarily employed _____ (herein after referred to as "Consultant") to assist me in the training of my dog(s) _____ .

**Professional Fees:**
Professional fees shall be $_____ per hour, with a minimum of ____ hour per visit. After the initial hour, time will accrue in quarter-hour increments. Fees are due at the end of each training session unless otherwise agreed upon by both parties. Client will be billed at ½ the normal appointment fee for any "no shows" or appointments canceled with fewer than 24 hours notice.

**Desciption of Services:**
I understand that the Consultant will work directly with me and my pet to impart contemporary animal behavior knowledge that best fits our needs, and that successful companion pet programs depend on a combination of learned skills on the part of the pet and owner. Behavior is not static; an animal will not continue to perform even trained behaviors without ongoing practice. Especially in cases involving any type of aggression, although behavior may be modified, the dog is never considered "cured." A pet's behavior is ultimately the owner's responsibility. Consultant will make every reasonable effort to help us attain goals but makes no guarantees of performance on the part of Client or pet as a result of providing professional animal behavior consultation.

Client acknowledges that obedience training/behavior modification may be an activity in which damage or injury to dog(s) and/or persons may occur. Client will assume full financial/moral responsibility for the actions of their dog(s). Client further acknowledges that dog(s) may be exposed to a variety of environmental conditions which include, but are not limited to, vehicular travel, interaction with people and other animals, exposure to adverse weather, and exposure to areas with crowds and all types of traffic.

I/We Client agree that I, my/our heirs, assignees and legal representatives will not make claim against, sue, or attach the property of Consultant, her family, acquaintances, or any other person acting on her behalf (herein referred to as "Her Agents"), for injury or damage done to or by dog(s) resulting from action or negligence, however caused, by Consultant or Her Agents. I/We Client forever release Consultant and/or Her Agents from any and all liability and demands which I/We Client, and my/our heirs, assignees and legal representatives may have or may hereafter have for injury or damage to or by dog(s), and assume all risks thereof.

Client and Consultant hereby agree to mediate and/or arbitrate any misunderstanding that may arise pursuant to the terms contained herein. In any action or proceeding arising out of this agreement, the prevailing party shall be entitled to reimbursement of costs and legal fees.

This Contract for Training Services supersedes all other agreements, written or oral, previously made between Client and Consultant.

Executed on this _____ day of _____, 2_____

       "Client"                                 "Consultant"

_____    _____
       (print name)

_____
       (signature)

## Positive Training Principles and Tips

Training your dog should be an enjoyable experience for you both. The more you understand about how your dog thinks and learns, the more effectively you can communicate. Clear communication means successful training and good behavior—with no need for force or coercion!

1. **Behavior that is rewarded is more likely to reoccur.** This powerful principle is a key component of reward-based training. *Dogs do what works.* If your dog receives praise and a treat for sitting, he is more likely to sit the next time you ask. If he knows that jumping on you will earn your attention, he will keep jumping, as attention is rewarding to him.

2. **Dogs learn by association.** When training, it is important that the reward closely follow the desired behavior. For example: when teaching your dog to sit, the praise and treat should be given when his rear touches the floor, not after he's stood up again. On the other side of the coin, reprimanding your dog for something he may have done hours ago (e.g., you come home to find your slippers shredded) is pointless. Your dog won't associate your yelling with what he's done, and if it happens often enough, he may begin to fear your arrival home, as you are always angry for no reason he can fathom.

3. **Reward behaviors you want, rather than punishing behaviors you don't want**. Most of us are so accustomed to noticing "mistakes" our dogs make that it seems strange to begin noticing and rewarding "good" behavior. For example: your dog barks, so you yell at him to be quiet. Sure, a barking dog is hard not to notice. But what about when he's lying calmly? Most of us never consider rewarding calm behavior, so the dog only gets rewarded with our attention (even yelling is attention) when he is doing something inappropriate. Having been rewarded, of course he keeps doing those things! Make a habit of noticing and rewarding your dog for good behavior.

4. **Extinction** *If a behavior is ignored, it will eventually extinguish on its own.* Imagine you are trying to buy a soda from a vending machine. You drop in your change, press the button, and wait. Nothing happens. You press the button more forcefully, and try a few others as well. Still nothing. You jangle the change lever. No soda, no change. You might even, at that point, shake or kick the machine. Finally, grumbling to yourself, you give up and leave. In this example, the soda-seeking behavior *extinguished* because there was no payoff, no reward. Kicking or shaking the machine is an example of an *extinction burst*. What that means with your dog is that if you ignore an unwanted behavior, it will eventually stop (unless it is something that is inherently self-rewarding to the dog, such as digging). But before your dog gives up, the behavior may actually escalate. Recognize the extinction burst for what it is, and wait it out—the behavior *will* eventually stop, and will stop even sooner the next time around.

5. **Positive reinforcement is something the dog wants**. Just because you think those expensive new treats are a great reward doesn't mean they are. If your dog turns his nose up at them, they're not much of a reward in his mind. A reward can be petting, verbal praise, a throw of the ball, a quick game with a favorite toy, sniffing grass, saying hello to another dog, etc. The sky's the limit. Consider what your dog finds rewarding, and use it!

6. **Jackpot!** *The jackpot is something really special, head and shoulders above the usual reward.* Your dog can earn this amazing prize by doing something especially wonderful. While it is always important to use training treats your dog likes, save the Super-Yummy, Best-Treat-In-The-World as a jackpot. For example, a dog knows what Sit means, but doesn't sit very quickly. When you give the sit cue, he watches you for a moment, then languidly lowers his butt to the floor. You can almost hear him sigh, "Okay, if I must." But on the fourth repetition, he responds immediately; butt hits floor in record time. Jackpot! You immediately give him one piece after another of the special treat, along with effusive praise (and petting, if he enjoys it). You can also give a mega-jackpot by tossing a shower of treats. Jackpotting makes an impression—it calls the dog's attention to the fact that he's done something wonderful. He is therefore more likely to perform the behavior better than usual the next time. A jackpot doesn't have to be food, either. If your dog lives for a toss of the ball or a game of tug, use that as your jackpot. Know your dog and use what works for him.

7. **Find an alternate behavior.** When you want your dog to stop doing something, give him something else to do that is incompatible with the behavior you don't want. For example: if your dog jumps on you, have him sit instead; he can't sit and jump at the same time. If he chews on furniture, give him an appropriate chew toy instead. Try this: On a piece of paper, draw a vertical line down the center. On the left, list all the things your dog does that you'd like him to stop doing. On the right, next to each behavior, write down something he could do instead. It's easy!

8. **Raise criteria gradually** in small increments, building on each success. Simply put, that means *don't expect too much too soon.* Instead, build small steps to get from Point A to Point B. For example: when teaching your dog to down-stay, start with a three-second down-stay. If that is successful, add two seconds, and so forth. Any time your dog does not perform an exercise correctly, consider whether you have proceeded too quickly. Go back to the point at which your dog was last successful, then build gradually. Setting your dog up to succeed eliminates the need for corrections.

9. **If trained correctly, behavior is not contingent on food being present.** This is something that many people who are opposed to food-reward training don't understand. If you phase treats out gradually and use lots of real-life rewards (petting, games, etc.) as well, your dog will do as asked even when no treats are present. Use a lot of treats at first to teach and then practice new behaviors. Eventually, rewards should become fewer and farther between—but they should not stop altogether. You wouldn't want to stop getting paid once you got better at your job, so don't forget to reward at times for a job well done!

10. **Training should be fun!**
- Keep training sessions short; 3-5 minutes a few times daily is fine.
- Focus on one behavior in each session.
- Keep an upbeat attitude when training. Don't train when you're cranky.
- End each training session on a successful note. Did your dog do seven good sits, with the last one being really great? End the session there.
- Once a new behavior has been learned, incorporate it into your daily routine.

**BE KIND TO YOUR DOG AND HAVE FUN TRAINING!**

# Leadership

Like children, dogs need guidelines and boundaries. Good leadership will earn your dog's respect and help him to feel secure. Here are a few ways to establish leadership:

1. *The Leader Controls The Resources.* Just as parents control allowance, curfew and use of the car, you should control all the "good stuff" when it comes to your dog.
- Food is an incredibly valuable resource. As such, it should come you, not from that round thing that is always magically full! Feed once or twice daily, rather than leaving food down. For dogs with severe leadership issues, or to kick-start your program, hand-feed meals (a few pieces at a time) for two weeks. Have your dog sit or perform another behavior for each bit of food.
- Control toys and games. Leave your dog with a few toys, but reserve the really special ones for when you are present. Bring these special toys out periodically and play with them, with your dog. Now you are also the source of all fun! *Note:* Playing tug is fine as long as you control the game, and your dog knows "Leave it". (If not, teach "Leave it" first.) Bring the toy out; initiate tug. Periodically freeze, followed by saying, "Leave it." When he releases, wait a beat, say, "Take it" and resume the game. (If at any time teeth touch skin, say, "Too bad!" Game over.) When you're finished playing, put the toy away where your dog can't get to it.

2. *Put Your Dog on a Learn to Earn Program.* That means your dog must do something in order to earn anything that is valuable to him. If your dog wants to be petted, ask him to sit first. If he's already sitting, ask him to lie down. Then pet. Have him sit (or perform another behavior) before meals, treats, walks, a toss of the ball, and anything else he finds valuable.

3. *Should you allow your dog on the furniture or your bed?* If there are no leadership issues and he will get down when asked, no problem! For dogs who are pushy and think they're in charge, no furniture/bed priveleges until leadership is better established, and then only when invited.

4. *Does your dog zig-zag in front when you walk, crowd you as you sit, or otherwise get in your space?* Not acceptable! For zig-zaggers, keep your feet firmly on the floor and shuffle right on through. Your dog will learn to move when human legs approach.If you are standing when your dog crowds you, use your lower body to gently push him away. If you are sitting, fold your arms and gently move him away using your upper arm or forearm—do not speak or look at him. At doorways,  either push him aside gently with your lower body or step in front to block his path. It is not always necessary for you to pass through doorways first, but shoving is not acceptable!

5. *Practice obedience exercises and incorporate them into your everyday life.* Down-stays are especially good for establishing leadership. Keep practice sessions short and frequent.

6. *Teach your dog to accept handling.* Do a daily massage that includes paws, ears and mouth. This practice also makes for easier groomer/vet visits and alerts you to any physical abnormalities.

7. *Good leaders are not bullies!* Reprimand verbally when necessary, then forgive and move on. Do not use harsh physical corrections. Use praise and rewards to let your dog know when he is doing the right thing. Above all, be a kind and patient leader!

# Introduction to Clicker Training

*Clicker training is a fun and effective way to teach obedience exercises, solve behavior problems, and even teach tricks!*

Clicker training has been used with marine mammals for years and is a clear, effective way to communicate with your dog. A clicker is a small plastic box with a metal tab that makes a clicking sound when pressed. The click acts as a marker, to let your dog know the exact moment he is doing what you want. Why would a dog care that you click? Because each click is followed by a treat! Dogs learn very quickly that click equals treat, so they try to figure out how to make us humans "click." Why click instead of shouting, "Eureka!" or "You've got it!"? Because a click is faster and more precise than words. And the click sounds the same each time the dog hears it, whereas our verbal tone varies.

There are various ways to get a dog to do something that will earn a click. *Luring* means leading a dog into position by having him follow something, normally a treat. *Shaping* means rewarding progressive bits of a behavior. For example, to get a dog to lie down from a sit, you might first click and treat for a slight dip of the head, then for the head lowered, then for one paw out, etc. until the dog was lying down. Luring and shaping are often combined. *Capturing* a behavior means clicking each time the dog happens to do it on his own. If you clicked and treated each time your dog made eye contact, your dog would soon be staring at you! Once your dog is consistently performing a behavior, the verbal cue (i.e. "Down") can be given just before the start of the behavior.

- If your dog is afraid of the click, muffle the sound at first by putting the clicker in your pocket or placing a piece of tape over the metal tab. Ballpoint pens also make soft clicks.
- Don't point the clicker at your dog—it's not a remote control. (Wouldn't *that* be nice!)
- The clicker should not be used to get your dog's attention.
- The timing of the click is important, but don't worry too much if your timing is off at first; it will get better as you practice. If you do click at the wrong time, the dog still gets the treat.
- Many kids are great at clicker training! But do not allow young children access to the clicker unless they are doing supervised training.
- If your dog performs a behavior especially well, click only once, but jackpot by giving a few treats in a row, along with enthusiastic praise (and petting, if the dog enjoys being petted).
- Keep practice sessions short. Aim for three to five sessions of three to five minutes daily. Break sessions into 30-second rounds; work on one behavior for 30 seconds, then play/pet for a few seconds and start again. Try to end each round and session on a good performance.
- Change undesirable behaviors by clicking good ones. For example, if your dog jumps on people, click him for having four paws on the floor or sitting instead. For a barking problem, click for silence, starting with one second of quiet and working your way up.
- When working on a behavior such as Sit or Down, after clicking, toss the treat a short distance away from your dog so he has to stand up to go get it. That sets him up for the next repetition.
- You do not have to carry a clicker all the time! Once a behavior has been put on a verbal cue, you're done using the clicker for that particular behavior.

# Crate Training

Crate training is the process of conditioning your dog to accept being in a crate. Although crating is most often used for housebreaking, properly introduced, a crate can also become your dog's safe haven and favorite hangout. Crating can be used for short periods for management (so your dog won't destroy things while unsupervised), safe transportation via car or plane, and for keeping a dog calm when ill or recovering from surgery. And crate training is not just for puppies—it works for adult dogs as well.

There are two common types of crate. One resembles a cage with metal bars, and can be folded down into a flattened suitcase shape. Some people prefer metal crates for heavy-coated breeds, since they offer better ventilation. The second type consists of a hard plastic snap-together top and bottom, with ventilated slats on the sides and a metal grille door. This type of crate provides more of a solid enclosure and is preferred by many pet owners. While a new, quality crate for a medium to large dog is not cheap, the investment is worthwhile. A damaged carpet alone would cost more than the crate!

Crate training works because dogs have an instinct not to soil in their own area. The crate should be just large enough for your dog to stand up and turn around in. If your dog is a puppy, do not buy a huge crate for him to grow into. All that room would defeat the purpose! You could purchase a puppy-sized crate now and a larger one when your pup is bigger. Or, choose one that comes with dividers so you can expand your puppy's space as needed.

Place a blanket or old sweatshirt with your scent on it in the bottom of the crate. This will help to make your dog feel comfortable and secure. Keep the crate where you want your dog to sleep, preferably by the side of your bed. It is best to keep him within hearing range so you will know if he needs to eliminate during the night. Besides, he will most likely prefer to be close to you—and a happy dog equals less whining. When you first introduce the crate, be sure the door is propped open so as not to swing shut by accident. If your dog doesn't go in to explore on his own, place a few treats or his meal inside. Do not force your dog into the crate. Progress gradually to shutting your dog in the crate with a stuffed Kong or chew bone. Ideally, your dog should have a few days to get used to the crate before being required to sleep inside it.

The first night you crate your dog, gently help him in if necessary, then softly close the door. It is perfectly normal for your dog to whine, bark, or even throw tantrums the first night in a crate. Do *not* reward this behavior by letting him out! Try simply ignoring him for a while. If he does not stop after a reasonable amount of time, say "no" and tap the top of the crate. (Just don't get into the cycle of him whining and you saying "no" each time, thereby reinforcing the behavior by responding to it.) Young pups will have to eliminate during the night. You will quickly come to recognize the difference between a normal whine and a need-to-urinate whine. If the whining is frantic, open the crate door, *pick your dog up if possible* (if he is too heavy to pick up, leash and fast-walk him), and bring him to the spot where you want him to eliminate. As he goes, praise him in a high, happy voice, then return him to the crate. Most dogs, especially adults, get used to this routine very quickly and sleep through the night without interruption.

First thing in the morning, open the crate door and bring your dog to the elimination spot. Don't forget the praise! It is not necessary to use treats to reward elimination, but if you choose to do so, give the treat immediately after your dog eliminates, instead of waiting until you are back in the house.

During the day, your dog must be supervised. To help keep him in your sight, your dog may be leashed to you, or tethered to a heavy piece of furniture in the room in which you are spending time. (You may use a leash as a tether by wrapping it around a furniture leg, slipping the clip through the loop and attaching it to your dog's regular buckle collar.) If you cannot keep an eye on your dog, he should be left in a penned or gated area (such as the kitchen with a baby gate across the entrance), or crated. *Refrain from letting your dog out of your sight, even for a moment.* Accidents happen quickly! Be sure to take your dog out periodically to eliminate. Young puppies might have to eliminate as frequently as every 20 minutes. For older pups, once per hour may be all that is needed. Set a timer to help you remember.

If you catch your dog starting to circle and sniff or squat, startle him with a handclap or a sharp verbal "Eh-eh!" and quickly bring him to the proper elimination spot. If he goes, praise! If you find an accident that has already happened, consider it your own mistake and quietly clean up. (Use an enzymatic cleaner such as *Nature's Miracle*™ on carpets.) A dog will not associate your scolding him with that mess on the floor if you are scolding him more than a few seconds after the fact. In addition to your regular elimination opportunities, be sure to take your dog out upon waking, after naps, after meals, after drinking water, after playtime, and before bed. That means going out there with him, as opposed to letting him out and assuming he's done his business. *Note*: Do not physically correct your dog, or "rub his nose in it." A well-timed verbal correction should be effective.

If you must leave the house for a short period, you may leave your dog crated (up to four hours is fine for a dog who can hold it that long). This will prevent housebreaking accidents as well as destruction. Leave a favorite toy or chew bone in the crate with him. Do not leave food or water in the crate. If you must leave your dog for a longer period, or your dog is unable to hold it for the amount of time you will be gone, leave him in a safe confinement area such as a gated-off kitchen or bathroom. (Use a gate across bathroom doors rather than shutting the door.) Set his bedding at one end and wee pads or another elimination surface at the opposite end of the area. Tip: Practice crating your dog with a yummy chew toy while you are home. That way he won't associate being crated only with your absence.

Gradually introduce your dog to all areas of the house, so he will eventually not need to be confined or supervised. For now, let your dog spend time in these new areas *with your supervision*. It is important to do this so your dog will slowly come to accept the whole house as his territory, and not soil indoors. In the meantime, close doors to bedrooms and other rooms to which you do not want your dog to have access.

Housebreaking can be a frustrating process, but hang in there! The more you are home to supervise and reinforce proper behavior, the faster your dog will catch on. Do not get frustrated and banish your dog to the back yard. In order to learn proper house behavior, he must spend time in the house. It is normal for things to improve, and then have an accident; a few more "good" weeks go by, then another accident. This is a normal progression, and you will soon have a completely crate trained, housebroken dog.

# Appendix B

# Compilation of History Questionnaires

(Aggression and Separation Anxiety questionnaires have been omitted, as they are listed in usable fashion in their respective chapters.)

# History Questionnaires

## Background

1. Where did the dog come from?

2. If known background, why was dog given up?

3. How long have you had the dog?

4. Have you had previous dog experience?

5. Why did you choose this particular breed?

6. Why did you choose this particular dog?

## Physical and Medical Issues

1. Who is your veterinarian?

2. Is the dog current on vaccinations?

3. When was the dog's last veterinary exam?

4. Does the dog have any known medical problems?

5. Is the dog on any type of medication?

6. Is the dog spayed/neutered?

7. Does the dog have any food allergies?

## Feeding, Treats and Chew Items

1.  What type of food is the dog being fed?

2.  What types of treats, cookies or chew items does the dog get, and how often?

3.  How many times a day is dog fed?

4.  If feeding on a schedule, at what hours is the dog fed?

5.  Does the dog eat right away and finish the entire meal?

6.  Where is the dog fed and who is nearby when he eats?

7.  Who does the feeding?

8.  Does the dog get "people food" and if so at what location?

## Logistics

1.  Where does the dog sleep?

2.  Is the dog allowed on the furniture?

3.  Where does the dog eliminate?

4.  Where is the dog kept when no one is home?

5.  For what period of time, on average, is the dog left alone?

6.  What percentage of time does the dog spend indoors versus outdoors?

## Training

1. Has the dog had any previous training? (Describe familiar cues, training methods and who did the training.)

2. What tricks does the dog know?

3. Describe how you reprimand, correct, or punish your dog for unwanted behavior, and give an example of the circumstances under which you might do so.

4. Describe how you reward your dog for good behavior.

5. Who will be responsible for training the dog?

## General Information

1. What would you most like to change about your dog's behavior? Name at least three things, in order of importance.

2. Is the dog housebroken? Crate trained?

3. What type of exercise does the dog receive?

4. Can you describe a typical day in the life of your dog?

5. What is the dog's favorite treat? Can you name two others he enjoys?

6. What is the dog's favorite toy or game?

7. What is the dog's favorite activity?

8. What is your dog's least favorite thing?

9. Can family members handle dog physically? Bathe? Trim nails?

10. Do you plan to do any type of competition, dog sports or therapy-related activities with your dog?

**Behavior Issues**

1. Can you describe the behavior?

2. What would you like the dog to do instead?

3. When did the behavior first manifest?

4. Were there any changes in the household at the time the behavior first manifested?

5. How often does the behavior occur?

6. Under what specific circumstances does the behavior occur?

7. In what location does the behavior occur?

8. Who is present when the behavior occurs?

9. Has the frequency of the behavior increased, decreased, or remained the same?

10. Has the intensity of the behavior increased, decreased, or remained the same?

11. When was the most recent incident?

12. What prompted you to seek help at this time?

13. What has been done so far to address the problem?

14. How much time and effort are you willing to spend on resolving this issue?

15. Have you considered the options should the issue not be solvable?

16. Can you offer any other information that might be helpful?

# Appendix C

# Furthering Your Education

## Schools, Train-the-Trainer Seminars
## and Internship Opportunities

Animal Haven University
Susan Smith
South Kortright, NY
607-538-9117
Sue@raising-canine.com

DogSense
Legacy Canine Behavior and Training/Terry Ryan
Sequim, WA
360-683-1522
www.legacycanine.com

Dogs of Course
Dana C. Crevling
(seminars throughout the U.S.)
508-529-3568
www.dogsofcourse.com

Peaceable Paws Trainer-in-Training Intern Academy
Pat Miller
Hagerstown, MD
423-326-0444
www.peaceablepaws.com

Raise with Praise
Paul Owens
Burbank, CA
1-800-269-3591
www.raisewithpraise.com

The San Francisco SPCA Academy for Dog Trainers
www.sfspca.org/academy/index.shtml
415-554-3095

St. Huberts Animal Welfare Ctr. (internships)
Pia Silvani, Director of Training & Behavior
973-377-0116
e-mail psilvani@sthuberts.org

Also, for various seminars:
*Puppyworks*
www.puppyworks.com
707-745-4237

## Online Courses

Cynology College School of Canine Behavioral Sciences
Founded by James O'Heare
www.cynologycollege.com

# Books and Videos for Trainers

Dogwise
1-800-776-2665
www.dogwise.com

Tawzer Dog Videos
Wide selection of conference and seminar videos on dog training,
behavior and health issues.
1-888-566-3003
www.tawzerdogvideos.com

# Suggested Reading/Viewing by Subject

Most of the following books and videos can be ordered through
Dogwise or Tawzer Dog Videos:

## Theory/Principles of Training & Behavior

*The Culture Clash*
Jean Donaldson
Oakland, CA: James & Kenneth, 1996 ISBN 1-888047-05-4

*Don't Shoot the Dog!*
Karen Pryor
New York, NY: Bantam, revised edition 1999 ISBN 0-553-38039-7

*Excel-erated Learning*
Pamela J. Reid, Ph.D.
Oakland, CA: James & Kenneth, 1996 ISBN 1-888047-07-0

## Training Basic Obedience

*Dog-Friendly Dog Training*
Andrea Arden
New York, NY: Howell Books, 1999 ISBN 1-582450099

*The Power of Positive Dog Training*
Pat Miller
New York, NY: Hungry Minds, Inc., 2001 ISBN 0-7645-3609-5

*The Dog Whisperer*
Paul Owens
Holbrook, MA: Adams Media Corp., 1999 ISBN 1-58062-203-8

## Clicker Training

*Click for Joy!*
Melissa Alexander
Waltham, MA: Sunshine Books, 2003 ISBN 1-890948-12-8

*The How of Bow Wow: Building, Proofing & Polishing Behaviors*
(video)
Virginia Broitman & Sherri Lippman, 2003

*Clicking with your Dog*
Peggy Tillman
Waltham, MA: Sunshine Books, 2000 ISBN 1-890948-05-5

## Dealing with Clients

*Dealing with People You Can't Stand*\*
Dr. Rick Brinkman & Dr. Rick Kirschner
US: McGraw-Hill, 1994 ISBN 0-07-007838-6

*Dog Behavior Problems: The Counselor's Handbook*
William E. Campbell
BehaviorxSystems, 1999 ISBN 0966870514

*Since Strangling Isn't an Option*\*
Sandra A. Crowe, M.A.
NY: Penguin Putnam Inc., 1998 ISBN 0-399-52540-8

*The Evans Guide for Counseling Dog Owners*
Job Michael Evans
New York, NY: Howell Book House, Inc., 1985 ISBN 0-87605-660-5

*It's Not the Dogs, It's the People! A Dog Trainer's Guide to Training Humans*
Nicole Wilde
Santa Clarita, CA: Phantom Publishing, 2003 ISBN 0-9667726-3-6

\* These books are not specifically aimed at dog trainers but apply nonetheless!

## Breed Characteristics

*The Irrepressible Toy Dog*
Darlene Arden
New York, NY: Howell Book House, 1998 ISBN 0-87605-649-4

*The Encyclopedia of Dog Breeds*
Juliette Cunliffe
New York, NY: Barnes & Noble, Inc., 2002 ISBN 0-7607-3458-5

*The Encyclopedia of the Dog*
Bruce Fogle, D.V.M.
New York, NY: Dorling Kindersley Publishing, Inc., 1995 ISBN 0-7894-0149-5

*Paws to Consider*
Brian Kilcommons & Sarah Wilson
New York, NY: Warner Books, Inc., 1999 ISBN 0-446-52151-5

*The Right Dog For You*
Daniel F. Tortora, Ph.D.
New York, NY: Simon & Schuster, Inc., 1980 ISBN 0-671-47247-X

## Canine (and Human) Body Language

*Dog Language*
Roger Abrantes
Napervielle, IL: Wakan Tanka, 1997 ISBN 0966048407

*How to Speak Dog*
Stanley Coren
New York, NY: Fireside, 2000 ISBN 0-684-86534-3

*Both Ends of the Leash* (seminar, 3-part video)
Patricia B. McConnell, Ph.D.
(Available through dogsbestfriendtraining.com)

*The Other End of the Leash*
Patricia B. McConnell, Ph.D.
U.S./Canada: The Ballantine Publishing Group, 2002 ISBN 0-345-44679-8

*The Body Language and Emotions of Dogs*
Myrna M. Milani, Ph.D.
Harper Collins, 1993 ISBN 0688128416

*On Talking Terms with Dogs: Calming Signals*
Turid Rugaas
Kula, HI: Legacy by Mail, Inc. 1997

## Behavior, Medical Issues, Protocols

*The Dog Who Loved Too Much*
Dr. Nicholas Dodman
New York, NY: Bantam Books, 1996 ISBN 0-553-10194-3

*Dogs Behaving Badly*
Dr. Nicholas Dodman
New York, NY: Bantam Books, 1999 ISBN 0-553-10873-5

*Pet Behavior Protocols: What to Say, What to Do, When to Refer*
Suzanne Hetts, Ph.D.
Lakewood, CO: AAHA Press 1999, ISBN 0-941451-74-7

*Applied Dog Behavior and Training* (Vols. 1-3)
Steven R. Lindsay
Vol. 1 – Principles of Adaptation Behavior and Learning
Ames, Iowa: Iowa State University Press, 1999 ISBN 0-8138-0754-9
Vol. 2 – Etiology and Assessment of Behavior Problems
Ames, Iowa: Iowa State University Press, 2001 ISBN 0-8138-2868-6
Vol. 3 – Procedures and Protocols
Ames, Iowa: Iowa State University Press, 2003 ISBN 0-8138-0738-7

*Clinical Behavioral Medicine for Small Animals*
Karen L. Overall
St. Louis, Missouri: Mosby, 1997 ISBN 0-8016-6820-4

## Aggression

*Aggression in Dogs*
Brenda Aloff
Colliervielle, TN: Fundcraft, Inc., 2002 ISBN 1-59196-073-8

*Dogs are From Neptune*
Jean Donaldson
Canada: Lasar Multimedia Prod., Inc., 1998 ISBN 0-9684207-1-0

*Mine!* (resource guarding)
Jean Donaldson
US: Kinship Communications, 2002 ISBN 0-9705629-4-2

*The Cautious Canine* (booklet)
Patricia B. McConnell, Ph.D.
Black Earth, WI: Dog's Best Friend, Ltd. 1998 ISBN 1-891767-00-3

*Dog-Dog Aggression* (3-part video)
Patricia B. McConnell, Ph.D.
www.dogsbestfriendtraining.com

*Feeling Outnumbered?* (managing a multi-dog household)
Patricia B. McConnell, Ph.D. & Karen B. London, Ph.D.
Black Earth, WI: Dog's Best Friend, Ltd., 2001 ISBN 1-891767-06-2

*Feisty Fido: Help for the Leash Aggressive Dog*
Patricia B. McConnell, Ph.D. & Karen B. London, Ph.D.
Black Earth, WI: Dog's Best Friend, Ltd. 2003 ISBN 1-891767-07-0

*The Canine Aggression Workbook*
James O'Heare, Dip.C.B.
Canada: Gentle Solutions, 2nd edition 2003 ISBN 0-9689668-4-5

*Dog to Dog Aggression* (video)
*Defensive Handling* (video)
*Possession and Food Bowl Aggression* (video)
Sue Sternberg
(available through www.suesternberg.com)

Also: see Overall's book, Lindsay's books, and Tawzerdogvideos.com
for seminar videos on dealing with aggression.

**Separation Anxiety**

*I'll Be Home Soon*
Patricia B. McConnell, Ph.D.
Black Earth, WI: Dog's Best Friend, Ltd. 2000 ISBN 1-891767-05-4

*Canine Separation Anxiety Workbook*
James O'Heare
Ottawa, Canada: DogPsych 2002, ISBN 0-9689668-3-7

Also: see Overall's book and Lindsay's books

## Other Publications

*The Whole Dog Journal*
Subscriptions 1-800-829-9165
Back issues 1-800-424-7887

## Web sites (Training & Behavior Issues)

*An Animal Trainer's Guide to Operant and Classical Conditioning*
(Stacy Breslau-Schneck)
www.wagntrain.com/OC/

*Behavior: Understanding and Modifying*
(articles by Cindy Tittle Moore)
www.k9web.com/dog-faqs/behavior.html

*Clicker Solutions Training Articles*
www.clickersolutions.com/articles/index.htm

*Dog Owner's Guide*
(breed profiles, training tips, health info, legal issues and more)
www.canismajor.com/dog/index.html

*Dr. P's Dog Training Library*
www.uwsp.edu/psych/dog/library.htm

*Flying Dog Press*
(articles by Suzanne Clothier)
www.flyingdogpress.com/articles.html

*Pet Behavior Resources*
(William E. Campbell)
www.webtrail.com/petbehavior/index.html

# Other Books by Nicole Wilde

## *So You Want to be a Dog Trainer*

A professional trainer shares advice, step-by-step instructions and inside secrets. Chapters include: Getting an Education; Setting up Your Business; Advertising; Group Classes; In-home Sessions; Difficult Clients; Trainer Etiquette; Products; more. 172 pgs.

*"Overflowing with useful information. A definite MUST-READ for any aspiring dog trainer!"*
- Jean Donaldson, author *The Culture Clash*

## *It's Not the Dogs, It's the People!*

A dog trainer's guide to positive training methods for humans. How to handle Angry Agnes, Unmotiated Mo, Know-It-All-Ned and other difficult personality types, in group classes and private lessons. 144 pgs.

*"Humorous, practical and ever so helpful, this book is a must-read for anyone who trains people to train dogs."* - Patricia McConnell, Ph.D.

*Living with Wolfdogs* offers invaluable information, whether you share your life with a wolfdog or are considering doing so. Packed with photos, advice, answers, tips and tricks. 104 pgs.

*Wolfdogs A-Z: Behavior, Training & More* is a comprehensive guide to training wolfdogs using positive, gentle methods. Includes step-by-step instructions and photos. Basic obedience; solutions to common behavior problems; clicker training; raw diet; health care; fear issues; dominance challenges; understanding body language; more. 268 pgs.

**Available through Dogwise at www.dogwise.com
(1-800-776-2665) or www.amazon.com**